Mental Health in Children and Young People

Sarah Vohra qualified at Leeds Medical School in 2008. She is a child psychiatrist based in the UK. Sarah is an author, columnist and blogger whose writings and work empower every single adult to recognize the early signs that a child may be struggling with his or her emotional or mental health. Like any disease, early recognition and intervention are key in mental illness, and Sarah's mission is to teach the simple strategies she uses in her everyday clinical practice so that any adult can gain the confidence to have a conversation with a potentially distressed child.

D1424052

Overcoming Common Problems Series

Selected titles

A full list of titles is available from Sheldon Press,
36 Causton Street, London SW1P 4ST and on our website at
www.sheldonpress.co.uk

Beating Insomnia: Without really trying
Dr Tim Cantopher

Chronic Fatigue Syndrome: What you need to know about CFS/ME
Dr Megan A. Arroll

Cider Vinegar
Margaret Hills

Coeliac Disease: What you need to know
Alex Gazzola

Coping Successfully with Hiatus Hernia
Dr Tom Smith

Coping with a Mental Health Crisis: Seven steps to healing
Catherine G. Lucas

Coping with Difficult Families
Dr Jane McGregor and Tim McGregor

Coping with Endometriosis
Jill Eckersley and Dr Zara Aziz

Coping with Memory Problems
Dr Sallie Baxendale

Coping with Schizophrenia
Professor Kevin Gournay and Debbie Robson

Coping with the Psychological Effects of Illness
Dr Fran Smith, Dr Carina Eriksen and Professor Robert Bor

Coping with Thyroid Disease
Mark Greener

Depression and Anxiety the Drug-Free Way
Mark Greener

Depressive Illness: The curse of the strong
Dr Tim Cantopher

Dr Dawn's Guide to Brain Health
Dr Dawn Harper

Dr Dawn's Guide to Digestive Health
Dr Dawn Harper

Dr Dawn's Guide to Healthy Eating for Diabetes
Dr Dawn Harper

Dr Dawn's Guide to Healthy Eating for IBS
Dr Dawn Harper

Dr Dawn's Guide to Heart Health
Dr Dawn Harper

Dr Dawn's Guide to Sexual Health
Dr Dawn Harper

Dr Dawn's Guide to Weight and Diabetes
Dr Dawn Harper

Dr Dawn's Guide to Women's Health
Dr Dawn Harper

The Fibromyalgia Healing Diet
Christine Craggs-Hinton

Helping Elderly Relatives
Jill Eckersley

How to Stop Worrying
Dr Frank Tallis

Invisible Illness: Coping with misunderstood conditions
Dr Megan A. Arroll and Professor Christine P. Dancey

Living with Fibromyalgia
Christine Craggs-Hinton

Living with Hearing Loss
Dr Don McFerran, Lucy Handscomb and Dr Cherilee Rutherford

Living with the Challenges of Dementia: A guide for family and friends
Patrick McCurry

Overcoming Emotional Abuse: Survive and heal
Susan Elliot-Wright

Overcoming Low Self-esteem with Mindfulness
Deborah Ward

Overcoming Worry and Anxiety
Dr Jerry Kennard

Post-Traumatic Stress Disorder: Recovery after accident and disaster
Professor Kevin Gournay

The Stroke Survival Guide
Mark Greener

Ten Steps to Positive Living
Dr Windy Dryden

Treating Arthritis: The drug-free way
Margaret Hills and Christine Horner

Understanding High Blood Pressure
Dr Shahid Aziz and Dr Zara Aziz

Understanding Yourself and Others: Practical ideas from the world of coaching
Bob Thomson

When Someone You Love Has Dementia
Susan Elliot-Wright

The Whole Person Recovery Handbook
Emma Drew

Mental Health in Children and Young People

Spotting symptoms and seeking help early

DR SARAH VOHRA

First published in Great Britain in 2018

Sheldon Press
36 Causton Street
London SW1P 4ST
www.sheldonpress.co.uk

The author and publisher have made every effort to ensure that the external website
and email addresses included in this book are correct and up to date at the time of
going to press. The author and publisher are not responsible for the content, quality or
continuing accessibility of the sites.

British Library Cataloguing-in-Publication Data
A catalogue record for this book is available from the British Library

ISBN 978–1–84709–469–8
eBook ISBN 978–1–84709–470–4

Typeset by Manila Typesetting Company
First printed in Great Britain by Ashford Colour Press
Subsequently digitally printed in Great Britain

eBook by Manila Typesetting Company

Produced on paper from sustainable forests

This book is for any adult who is worried about a child's emotional or mental health.

I also wish to dedicate the book to my daughter Amelie and husband Ravi, whose love and support throughout the whole writing process have been immeasurable.

Contents

Note to the reader

The words 'parent' and 'carer' are used interchangeably within the text. While the book primarily addresses parents and carers, it is designed to be of use to anyone concerned about a child's mental health, whether a grandparent, teacher, social worker, police officer, sports coach and so forth. This book is not intended as a substitute for medical advice; in the event of concern, you should consult your doctor.

Introduction

We hear a great deal at the moment about mental health and the need to change the conversation around it; everyone, from celebrities and politicians to royals, is advocating that there needs to be more openness and less shame when it comes to sharing our emotional difficulties. We know ourselves, as adults, only too well how much of a struggle the prospect of opening up to people can be, yet we expect our children to be entirely open and honest in their communication with us.

Parenting throws many challenges our way. As my daughter gets older, I have found myself anxiously anticipating the difficulties she may face and possibly have to overcome: peer pressure bullying, body image issues and eating difficulties, to name but a few. While at the moment she is far from shy about vocalizing when she is or isn't happy about something or when she does or doesn't want to do something, I worry that there will come a time when communicating with me will feel too challenging or too difficult a hurdle for her to overcome. I worry that I will know deep down that something is the matter but will be rendered powerless by the shrugged shoulders or closed bedroom door.

As a child psychiatrist, I empathize only too well with the frustration and helplessness you may feel when you find yourself sitting in front of a child who refuses to open up to you. You never know how far to push it in such a situation. You worry that by doing so you will make things worse or it will open up a can of worms you have no idea what to do with. You worry that you are overthinking things or overreacting to something that is probably just a normal part of growing up. You feel that, as a parent, you ought to be able to handle it and you will be judged by others for admitting defeat and asking for help. Maybe you have got as far as taking your child to the GP or to A&E, but feel that you may as well have not bothered. You've been told to keep an eye on things and bring the child back if necessary, only to land up in the same situation as before, with your offspring still not talking to you and the problems seemingly getting worse.

What then? You may have been referred to a mental health specialist – finally, a light at the end of the tunnel – only to be told that it could be several months, maybe even a year, before your child is assessed. You end up feeling exasperated by the whole process. In among all that, you may turn in desperation to your favourite 'search engine doctor' to give you the answers you need – 'How do I get my child to open up? How do I stop my child self-harming? Why is my child losing weight?' – but feel overwhelmed by the thousands of hits, leaving you feeling panicked and none the wiser.

The idea of this book came from my personal and professional experience of speaking to parents – parents who have struggled to manage their children's emotional difficulties – and listening to their frustrations of not having had professional, specialist advice to hand earlier or in one place or of having had to wait several months before beginning to access it. With this in mind, I wrote a list of all the common mental health issues that I am faced with from day to day. I set about creating a resource that would be informative and understandable, but also practical. To make it simpler to understand each condition, I broke the information down into bite-size chunks, looking at each potential symptom in turn. Not only did I want to focus on how to spot symptoms (the premise of the book was borne out of parents not really knowing what to do beyond that) but I also wanted to instil in parents the confidence to take action to help their child.

To make this process easier, I introduced a 'traffic light' system of action – an approach I use within my own clinical practice with parents and young people alike. There may be times when a simple conversation with your child may be enough to settle his or her distress or anxiety. At other times, you may need to get support from a healthcare professional, such as a GP, so that a more thorough assessment can be completed. There may be times when you categorically feel unable to manage your child's difficulties and worry that she is at serious risk of hurting herself or potentially others, and you may have to take your child straight to A&E or even contact emergency services for a more urgent assessment. The step-by-step traffic light system will, I hope, simplify your decision-making and empower you to take the most appropriate action.

Throughout the book, I make reference to the 'parent' or 'carer', but, in fact, this text will be an invaluable resource for any adult who is concerned about a child's mental health: siblings, extended family, friends, teachers, social workers and even sports coaches, to name but a few, will all stand to benefit from the advice shared. In an average waking day, your child may well come into contact with lots of people, so it is important that all feel prepared and emotionally available, in equal measure, to take on whatever comes their way.

This book is not intended to replace or be a substitute for the medical advice of your doctor or healthcare provider, but what I hope it will do is equip any adult, no matter their relationship with the child, their qualification or profession, whether he or she has known the child for years or they have only just met for the first time, with the tools needed to spot early warning signs of mental health difficulties, have a confident conversation with that child early on and to access professional support sooner rather than later.

1

'Let's talk': getting the conversation started

Being a parent can be a rewarding but very challenging experience. From a crying baby, then tantruming toddler to sulky teenager, you can generally tell when your child is unhappy about something. You are also fairly likely to be clued up on what to do when your child is physically unwell and perhaps throwing up, with a sore tummy or full of cold. We know what we can manage ourselves at home and what may require a trip to the GP or even to A&E. However, most of us are less confident when it comes to managing our children's emotional problems. This could be anything from exam pressures to your child's first heartbreak. It is sometimes difficult to know what the right thing to say is, if anything at all.

When it comes to emotional stress, we are reliant on our children to tell us how they feel. What makes it all the harder is that children with mental health difficulties may struggle to realize themselves that there is anything wrong, or may not be willing to admit as much. They can often feel a real sense of shame or fear asking for help, even from those closest to them. The fact that their symptoms are not immediately obvious to the naked eye means that such children's difficulties can remain under the radar for some time before you get wind of them. You may not find out about your child's problems until the child has reached a crisis point and can no longer keep a lid on things.

Understanding your child's mental health problems

Parents and carers often struggle to understand mental health difficulties such as anxiety, particularly if there is seemingly no trigger for them. If your child falls over and cuts her leg open, it is easy as a parent to empathize with her pain and understand why she might be a bit upset. However, it can be really difficult to show the same level of understanding for your child's mental health difficulties.

There are many factors that can get in the way of discovering your child is struggling with his or her mental health. Let's now try to unpick some of these communication barriers.

Your child may be thinking:

'I don't want to upset my mum and dad.'
'They will feel guilty and blame themselves.'
'They will be angry with me.'
'They are too busy.'
'They will be ashamed.'

The parent may think:

'I'm worrying about nothing.'
'It's just a phase.'
'What if I make things worse?'
'I may not be able to deal with it emotionally.'
'This is all my fault.'

To put this into context and highlight the common obstacles faced by parents, I'm going to use the case of Charlie as an example. It is written through the eyes of Charlie's mum, Rachel.

Charlie, 13

I'm worried about Charlie. He seems sadder than usual. He is always jumping down our throats over silly little things. I'm worried he isn't eating either. I've already asked him, quite a few times actually, if everything is OK. He tells me he's fine and shuts down any attempt at a conversation afterwards. Perhaps this is normal teenage behaviour? I took him to see the GP, but he reassured me there wasn't anything to worry about. He just told me to keep an eye on things and bring him back if he gets any worse. I've asked Charlie how things have been since we went to see the GP and he shouted at me. I've decided to leave him be for now, it is not worth getting into another argument over.

We are a few months on now and I guess you could say we've left things on the back burner for now. He seemed all right and until recently I thought we might have turned a corner, but now his sleep is suddenly all over the place. He spends so much time in his bedroom and I'm never quite sure what he gets up to in there. Nothing could have prepared me for what I saw last Saturday afternoon. As I flung his bedroom door open, I was half expecting to find him on his headset, playing a computer game with his virtual friends. Instead, I caught him sat on his bed with a glass of water in one hand and an empty box of paracetamol in the other; he told me he had taken the lot.

Recognizing the problem: trusting your gut

By the time a concerned parent or adult goes to see her GP, she may have a clear timeline in her mind of when her child's difficulties started and how they have developed since. The parent may have come to her own understanding of what is going on. More often than not, in the first instance, she may try to normalize it.

> 'I'm worrying about nothing.'
> 'He's just being a typical teenager.'
> 'He would tell me if there was something wrong.'

Looking back at the case study, you can see why Rachel would assume that Charlie's behaviour is just that of your average teenager. How many teenagers do you know who are short-tempered, camp out in their rooms and are fussy with their eating?!

Accessing support

One of the things we do as parents when we first notice that something is wrong is to set ourselves a vague time limit as to when to get help.

> 'If it carries on for another week, then I'll go and see the GP.'
> 'If this rash doesn't clear up by the end of the day, then I'll ...'

Parents often worry that they will be seen by their GP or healthcare professional as time-wasters or, worse still, 'that overly anxious parent'. As a psychiatrist, it is interesting for me to observe the different stages at which parents ask for help. Some parents or concerned adults may ask for help from the off, when they *first* notice the change in mood or behaviour. Others may not do so until they have found their child at his or her most vulnerable or distressed, for example when they have caught the child self-harming for the first time. The one question you should ask yourself, when thinking about your child's difficulties is 'What does your gut say?'

Gut instinct

Gut instinct is the most undervalued tool you own as a parent. You can't replicate parental instinct. If your gut is telling you to be worried, be worried. Don't ignore your concerns or try to play them down. Have that first conversation with your child early on and seek professional advice and support as soon as possible.

When should I talk to my child?

It can be really difficult, as a parent, to decide whether it is the right time to talk to your child about your worries. Thinking back to our case study, this was something that Rachel really struggled with. There never seemed to be a right time to do it and when she did eventually pluck up the courage to speak to Charlie, he shut her down straight away.

Before having that conversation with your child and sharing your concerns with him, ask yourself these three key questions. An easy way to remember them is by using the abbreviation TLC.

- Is this the most appropriate **T**ime to have the conversation?
- Is this the most appropriate **L**ocation to have the conversation?
- Is this right way to talk to this **C**hild?

Timing the conversation

The timing of your conversation is hugely important. Don't rush your child, and make sure you give her your full attention. Clear your diary and think about possible distractions; switch your phone off if you're likely to get texts, calls and so on. Have the conversation at a time when you are least likely to be disturbed by others.

Location

Where you have the conversation is just as crucial as the timing of it. Trying to talk over the dining table, in front of the rest of the family, is unlikely to be appropriate. Your child may not want her siblings to know the ins and outs of what is happening, regardless of how well they get on. Similarly, try to avoid public places such as busy coffee shops and restaurants where the child will be conscious that other people may be listening in.

Pick a location and ask your child if she is happy for you to chat there. If not, ask the child where she would be more comfortable. Where you have the conversation may be different from one child to the next. The age of your child can often be a huge factor in this. For Rachel, she may consider having the conversation in Charlie's bedroom, particularly if that is where he is spending most of his time. If your child is a bit younger, he may prefer to be out in the garden or chat to you in his makeshift den.

Whatever the options, let your child take the lead in where to have the conversation. If he is comfortable in his environment, it may make opening up that bit easier for him.

What is the right approach for your child?

Once you have decided on when and where to have the conversation, ask yourself if this is the *right way* to have the conversation. What works for one child will not necessarily work for others. What works for a 6-year-old will not necessarily work for a 16-year-old. If you force your child to sit down and fire a load of questions at him, you may lose him within the first couple of minutes. If you let your child take the lead, however, perhaps by picking an activity that you can both do together, even something as simple as going for a walk, you may hold his attention long enough to find out what's going on. Being informal and not making it too obvious that you are digging for information is an approach that works well for some children.

Sometimes watching your child play can be a good conversation starter. If the child is frantically throwing paint at a canvas or pulling limbs off her Barbie or Action Man, you might reflect your observations back to her:

'You seem really angry, is everything all right?'

How should I talk to my child?

Parents often struggle with *how* they should go about having the conversation itself. Many worry that they will get flustered, lose their train of thought and not put across everything that they planned to. As a mum, I love a checklist. Being able to tick things off as I go is quite satisfying and I think having a similar sort of structure when holding a difficult conversation can be very helpful. Most parents find that this helps them organize their thoughts, keeps them on track and makes sure all the important points are covered, while helping to prevent the conversation becoming fraught with anxiety and panic. It may suit many parents to write down everything they want to talk about. Others may be able to hold their checklist in mind and virtually tick off each point in turn; it all comes down to personal preference. That being said, it is not essential to have a list, and it isn't always practical.

To checklist or not to checklist?

Important as it may be to have a structure to your conversation, don't follow the structure at the expense of letting your child open up to you. If your child is telling you something, listen. Don't shut him down or steer him through your own agenda. The most valuable information that I will hear from any child is the information he or she *wants* to tell me – that is, the stuff the child says without having to be asked a question.

Getting it right: FACE-FEAR

As a professional, the question I'm asked most often is, 'How do I get my child to open up more readily?' While there is no secret formula, in my personal experience, I have found the following structure to be quite effective. I have developed the mnemonic FACE-FEAR, which I hope will be a useful tool for any parent or concerned adult wanting to talk to their child:

- talk **F**ace to face
- be **A**ttentive (listen)
- stay **C**alm
- **(E)**
- **F**acts
- **E**xplain
- **A**gree an Action
- **R**eview

FACE-FEAR – an explanation

F is for face to face

Wherever possible, try to have a conversation with your child face to face. Obviously this may not always be practical and you may need to be flexible in how and when you speak to the child. The mnemonic TLC, discussed earlier in this chapter, will help you to gauge when, where and how you talk to your child.

A is for being attentive or active listening

Tempting as it is to rush in with your own worries, give your child the opportunity to speak first. It may be that she has nothing to say to you, but at least you have given her a chance to speak free from any influence. If you sense that she needs some encouragement to open up, ask her an open-ended question - that is, a question which forces your child to answer with some detail. In contrast, a closed question is one where your child can only answer with a simple 'Yes' or 'No'.

If your child isn't being particularly talkative, asking her a closed question, like the examples given below, will only get you as far as a yes or no answer, which stops any conversation you may have planned in its tracks.

'Are you OK?'
'Are you enjoying school?'
'Has everything been OK in the last few months?'

However, there are ways you can ask the same questions that will encourage your child to give you a bit more information.

'What have you been up to today?
'What have you been up to at school?
'What have you been up to over the last few months?'

Active listening

- Make sure you acknowledge what your child has told you, if anything.
- Support and encourage the child as she is opening up, if you get the sense that she wants to offload.
- Praise the child for her honesty.
- If your child hasn't said very much, reflect this back to her: 'You seem quiet . . . You haven't said much this evening.' It is important that you acknowledge the silences, particularly if they are out of character.
- Tell the child why you are taking an interest: 'I just wanted to check everything was OK because I have been worried about you for a few days/weeks/months.'
- Ask the child whether there was anything else that she wanted to talk to you about.
- Remind the child that you are always here for her.

C is for staying calm

It can be all too tempting to start the conversation in a flurry of panic, upset and anger, depending on the situation you are faced with, but it is important that you remain calm.

You need to instil confidence in your child that you are able to take on whatever problem she throws at you. Sitting in front of the child, snapping, before she has had a chance to speak, or crying and begging her to be open with you, may cause the child to clam up.

Some children describe feeling guilty that they have upset their parents or they may even feel anger towards them for how their mum or dad has reacted to what they have said:

'I don't like upsetting my mum. She only gets upset when I am upset.'

'Dad just gets angry when I try to explain why I am smoking cannabis, so what is the point?'

Keeping calm

- Take a deep breath.
- Stick the kettle on.
- Meditate.
- Do whatever you need to do to relax.
- Go in there with a calm head on your shoulders.

F is for facts and E is for explain

It is important, as a parent, that you are able to point out to your child exactly what it is you are worried about. You may have observed changes in your child's mood and behaviour that concern you. Your observations are what we refer to as 'the facts'. As well as pointing these out, it is important that you explain why they worry you. The explanation part is really important as it puts your worries into context. It allows you to show your child why her behaviour is concerning you and, crucially, how it has changed from before.

'I have noticed that you are snapping at me more recently [fact]; we used to always get on so well [explain].'

'You aren't eating as much as you used to [fact]. You barely touched your breakfast/lunch/dinner [fact]. That's not like you - normally you can't get enough of your food [explain].'

'You aren't sleeping so well and you are always so tired in the day [fact]. You used to sleep like a baby - I would always have a job trying to get you up of a morning! [explain].'

No one likes to be confronted with their difficulties head on, least of all your child. He may not be ready to face them. He may get defensive or try to justify his behaviour. This may stop in its tracks any attempt to talk about what's happening. Alternatively, he may recoil and withdraw. Whatever your child's response, try to avoid being confrontational; the last thing you want is for the conversation to escalate into an argument. Get your concerns across as clearly but as sensitively as you can.

Avoiding being at loggerheads

- Make sure to acknowledge what your child has told you.
- Repeat this back to the child to ensure you have understood correctly what he is saying. This tells your child 'I am listening to what you have said and I have taken it on board.' There is nothing worse than your child feeling that he is not being listened to or his worries are not being taken seriously.
- If, after hearing the child out, you are still worried, tell him that. You are expecting your child to be honest with you, so it is important you mirror that honesty, such as, 'I know you said you are fine, but I am still really worried.'

A is for agree an action

Once you have worked your way through the first four stages, you need to think about what you are going to do with the information you have gathered. Make sure you include your child in this action stage. As much as possible, you want her to be on board with the plan. Seek her opinion. What does she think would help? Ask if she thinks speaking to someone outside the family, such as your GP or another healthcare professional, would be helpful.

Be prepared for the possibility that, even at this stage, your child may continue to deny that there is a problem. Be honest if you feel that you are coming up against some resistance. Let your child know that you are still worried and give her advance warning of what to expect. The last thing you want is for your child to feel that you have bulldozered in without considering how she may be feeling.

'I know you said that everything was fine and you don't need any help, but I am still worried. Shall we see how you get on over the next few days or weeks, and if things don't get any better we'll go and see the GP?'

This lets your child know that you are taking things seriously, but also prepares him for what may happen so it doesn't come as too much of a shock.

You may suggest that, until then, your child check in with you daily.

> 'How about we agree to have a quick five-minute catch-up at the end of each day to see how you are feeling?'

R is for review

The 'review' entails you making sure that, once you and your child agree to a plan, you:

- stick to it;
- go back to it and make sure you have both done what you have said you were going to do.

When you are checking in with your child, remind yourself of the acronym FACE-FEAR and use this as a structure for your review. Stay calm, listen and ask your child:

> 'How have things been since we last spoke a few days ago?'
> 'What are the positives?'
> 'What hasn't gone so well?'

Remember to listen to your child's responses rather than immediately launch in with your own opinion of how you think things have gone.

If you have agreed something with your child, try wherever possible to stick to it. Avoid constantly shifting the goalposts. If you do go back on your word, make sure you communicate your reasons for doing so clearly with your child.

> 'I know we agreed that we would only see the GP if things didn't get better, but I think it would still be helpful to talk with her about this last week/month to see what she thinks.'

Try to maintain open, honest communication. Your child may not like the idea of being dragged to the GP, particularly if, from his point of view, there is nothing to worry about, but at least you will have been upfront about things. Thrusting a last-minute GP appointment on your child may lead him to feel resentful and mistrust you.

One thing to bear in mind when having these conversations is that you shouldn't expect to receive all the information in one sitting. You may have to sit your child down a few times before she even begins to open up. You may be fed information in dribs and drabs. You may find that the style of your conversation changes from one day to the next. Some days a face-to-face chat may work better, at other times it may be a conversation by text. Your child may be a closed book one day, while on another he is more than happy to speak to you and offload. The point is to try to avoid throwing in the towel and giving up when faced with the first hurdle.

FACE-FEAR – a recap

F   **F**ace to face.
A   Be **A**ttentive – what does your child think has gone well since you last spoke, what is not so good?
C   Remember to stay **C**alm.
F   **F**acts – how do you think things have been since you last spoke?
E   **E**xplain why you are worried, if you still are.
A   **A**gree to follow through on the **A**ction agreed in the last conversation.
R   **R**eview.

What if my child won't communicate?

There are other ways in which your child can indicate her emotional state to you that don't necessarily require her to talk about her difficulties at length. Encourage your child to write down or draw an image of her difficulties, if she feels able to. Often using visual cues in the form of a traffic light system may be more practical.

A traffic light system is helpful for:

- **your child** it's a quick way for the child to let others know that he is struggling; it avoids the child needing to have an in-depth conversation about his difficulties when he may not be in the right headspace for such a thing;
- **parents** it gives you a snapshot of how your child is feeling at any given moment, particularly at times when she is refusing or struggling to open up verbally.

The traffic light system – what do the colours mean?

Green 'I am having a good day. I am managing my emotions well. I am feeling positive. I don't have negative thoughts about myself or thoughts about wanting to hurt myself or end my life. If I do get these thoughts, they are only in passing and I have no intention of acting on them.'

Amber 'I am finding things difficult at the moment. I think you need to sit down and talk to me. I have dark thoughts in my head about wanting to hurt myself, but I don't think I will do anything at the minute. I am just worried that if I don't talk to you about them, my thoughts will get stronger, I might move up to a red and do something to hurt myself. I may need to see a doctor.'

Red 'I am really struggling at the moment. I am finding it difficult to control my emotions - the thoughts in my head are getting darker and stronger. I have thoughts about wanting to harm myself and wanting to end my life. I need you to sit down and talk to me. It might be that I don't want to talk to you and you may need to ring the GP, call emergency services or take me to A&E for some advice.'

The methods

There are different ways to incorporate a traffic light system of communication. Here are just a few examples.

Traffic light cards

Give your child three pieces of card, cut to the size of playing cards: a red one, a yellow one and a green one. Encourage your child to hold a card out in front of her so that it is clearly visible to you whenever she wants to show how she is feeling. Your child may even put the card outside her bedroom door at the start and end of each day. If you are concerned about your child, use the FACE-FEAR approach to find out more information. If she clams up, ask her to show you a card in the colour that most accurately reflects her mood instead. If your child is a bit younger, maybe use smiley faces as an indicator: a sad face on red paper, a neutral face (a straight-line mouth) on yellow paper and a happy face on green paper.

Bracelets or rings

Using different-coloured pieces of jewellery as an indicator of distress often works better for children who find holding up cards too onerous or too bold an approach. Get your child three pieces of string or ribbon (one red, one yellow and one green) and cut to wrist circumference size. If your child wishes, she may want to buy ready-made bracelets or even rings in all three colours and change them at various times of day depending on her mood.

Sending a text or emoji

This approach works well for children who struggle to spend time with other people, including family. They may prefer their own company and spend prolonged periods in their bedroom. This method can also be helpful when used in conjunction with the suggestions above, as it allows you to check in with your child when he is out with friends or at school. Unless your child is within sight 24 hours a day, it can be difficult to stick 100 per cent with coloured cards or jewellery.

You may choose to do this in a number of ways. Your child may be able to fully articulate her difficulties to you in a text message. Some children may find this difficult and prefer to give you a quick sign that indicates they are struggling, such as by sending an emoji. Agree with your child which emojis would be most suitable and discuss with her what each would represent in terms of her level of distress. You could use:

- coloured heart emojis in red, yellow or green
- faces – smiley, straight or tearful
- hands with thumbs up, neutral or thumbs down.

Before using a traffic light system, it is important to be clear what each colour or emoji represents and what your response on seeing a particular colour or emoji may be. Have a conversation with your child. What do the colours red, yellow or green mean to him? For instance, your child holding up a red card or wearing a red ribbon could indicate that he is really struggling with his emotions and is in imminent danger of harming himself. As a parent, your response to seeing the red ribbon may be to have an initial conversation with your child about his mental health, before urgently booking him in to see the GP or even taking him straight to A&E.

At the end of most chapters within this book you will find, arranged according to the traffic light system, a checklist of actions you may take as a parent that are specific to your child's symptoms.

Table 1 Communication checklist

		Yes	*No*
1	Is your gut telling you to worry?		
2	Have you turned off any distractions?		
3	Is this the right time?		
4	Is this the right place?		
5	Is this the right way?		
6	Are you calm?		
7	Are you listening to what your child is saying?		
8	Have you got the facts?		
9	Have you explained your worries?		
10	Have you and your child agreed an action?		
11	Have you reviewed your action plan?		
12	Have you introduced a traffic light system of communication?		

Dr Vohra's take-home messages

- Don't underestimate the power of gut instinct.
- Think about the barriers - that is, the things that might get in the way of having a conversation.
- Before speaking to your child, ask yourself if this is the right time, the right location and the right approach for him or her (TLC).
- Use FACE-FEAR as the basis for that first conversation.
- Stay calm, listen to what your child has to say, get the facts, explain your concerns, agree an action and then review.
- If your child is finding it difficult to open up verbally, encourage her to utilize a traffic light system to indicate to you when she is OK and when she is struggling.

2

'I'm worried my child is depressed'

Charlotte, 13
I can't stop crying. Everything upsets me at the minute. Mum keeps asking me if I'm OK and I tell her that I'm fine. She won't understand. What have I got to feel down about at the end of the day? I've got better at hiding things from her. I spend my break times at school crying in the toilet just so no one will see me upset. My grades haven't slipped, which is surprising really, given I can't concentrate as well. Everything goes over my head and I can't seem to take anything in. My friends tell me I'm 'not with it' half the time. I haven't been replying to their texts or returning their phone calls. I just don't feel up to talking to anyone. I feel so isolated. Even playing hockey seems too much like hard work; I used to love playing after school. I just don't have the energy for it any more. I've been told I'll be lucky to make the first team again this year.

Tell-tale signs that your child is struggling with her mood

Feeling down, having no energy and struggling to enjoy things are just some of the symptoms of depression your child may experience. Your child may be able to recognize these symptoms herself and so come forward to tell you about them; what is more common though is that, as her parent or carer, you will notice the changes in the child's mood and behaviour first.

Looking back at our case study, Charlotte's mum clearly had concerns about her. As her mum, she may have noticed that Charlotte:

- appears sadder than normal;
- doesn't have much drive to do things any more;
- has suddenly lost interest in things she used to really enjoy, like playing hockey.

We all go through phases in life of feeling down, tired and lacking interest, and our children are no different. A common worry for parents is how they can work out when their child's low mood is more than just part and parcel of growing up. When should they worry that their child may *actually* be depressed? The box below and Table 2 on page 23 summarize what a parent may notice.

When you first take your child to the doctor with concerns about his mood, often your doctor will want to find out how long the low mood has lasted and how it affects your child's day-to-day life. If the symptoms have gone on longer than two weeks and are beginning to get in the way of different aspects of the child's

The three key or 'core' symptoms of depression

1 Low mood
What you as a parent may notice.
- You may notice that your child looks down a lot of the time.
- Your child may be more tearful than normal.
- Your child may tell you directly that he is feeling upset.
- You may notice that nothing seems to pick up your child's mood. You may do something together as a family and find he struggles to crack a smile.

2 Low energy
What you as a parent may notice.
- Your child may look shattered or drained.
- Your child may tell you that she feels tired all the time.
- The child may struggle to get up and have no drive.
- Everything the child does seems as though it requires a lot of effort.

3 No enjoyment
What you as a parent may notice.
- You may notice that the child struggles to smile or can't join in when everyone else is having a laugh or a giggle.
- Your child may be dropping out of school clubs that she used to enjoy.
- Your child may suddenly not be interested in things that she used to really enjoy.
- You might notice that your child is spending more time at home and making excuses not to go out and see friends.

life – things like family relationships, friendships, school or work – then this could be a possible sign of depression.

In our case study, Charlotte is clearly feeling upset and unhappy. She hasn't got the energy to run around the hockey pitch and has lost interest in and passion for the game.

Other symptoms of depression

As well as low mood, low energy and lack of enjoyment, here are some of the other symptoms you should look out for if you are concerned your child is depressed.

Difficulty concentrating

When your child is depressed, one of the things that can be affected is his concentration. School report cards and feedback from your child's teacher can be an invaluable resource. Your child may find it difficult to take in what is being said to him in the classroom. He may be easily distracted by his thoughts and forget what instructions the teacher has given him. At home, you may find your child seems more forgetful than normal and that you are having to repeat things over and over again. You may notice, when you are out and about, that he is not concentrating on what he is doing or where he is going.

You are no doubt aware that as children grow up and become more independent, their attention may become more selective; in other words they pick and choose what they listen to. A common dilemma for parents can be trying to work out what is normal and what is down to illness. So think about whether your child's symptoms are a change from the norm. For instance, if she is normally happy and outgoing and more recently she has been withdrawn and tearful, then this will almost certainly ring alarm bells. It is very important not to look at any of these symptoms in isolation. Put the symptom in the context of what else is going on. So, rather than jumping to the assumption that your child is depressed just because she has lost interest in something, look at what other symptoms she is experiencing and what else is going on around her.

Difficulty concentrating

What you as a parent may notice.
- You may find that your child's school grades are slipping.
- You may get feedback from your child's teachers that he can't seem to focus.
- You might find that (more so than usual!) he is not paying attention to what you tell him.
- Your child may seem 'away with the fairies' a lot of the time.
- Your child may have 'near misses' – for example, failing to pay attention when crossing the road and almost getting run over.

Withdrawal and isolation

In our case study, Charlotte also describes feeling isolated. She is making excuses not to see her friends.

You may notice your child distancing herself from friends and family. What starts out as a few excuses here and there may lead to her complete withdrawal from any form of social contact whatsoever. This tends to make the child feel more isolated, which in turn can make her feel more depressed.

Withdrawal and/or isolation

What you as a parent may notice.
- Your child may not want to get involved with family activities.
- The child seems to make excuses not to go out and see her friends.
- The child seems to be doing less generally, and may spend longer periods of time shut off in her bedroom than usual.
- Your child may find it difficult to leave the house.

Poor sleep

Problems with sleep can be another sign that your child is struggling with his mood. Your child's sleep can be affected in a number of ways. It may be that he is struggling to get off to sleep. He may be tossing and turning, and find it difficult to get comfortable. He may lie awake going over things in his head time and time again. He may find it difficult to switch off. Sometimes children with low mood find it hard to stay asleep once they fall asleep. They may wake up several times in the night for no particular reason and find it difficult to settle back to sleep. Some children may be up for an hour or two - even, in some cases, all night. Some children may find that they are waking up early in the morning, such as at 4 or 5 a.m., and struggling to nod off again.

Your child may struggle in some, if not all, of these areas. In some cases, your child's sleep pattern may be reversed. This means that she spends most of the day asleep and as a result is awake for most of the night. You may even worry that your child is sleeping too much.

Poor appetite

Changes in your child's appetite can also be indicative of depression. When your child is depressed, he may go off his food. You may notice that he is barely touching his meals and is pushing food around his dinner plate. Packed lunches may come back untouched. It may be that you don't appreciate the loss of appetite until you start to see changes in your child's weight; he may have lost a lot of weight in a short space of time. For some children it may be the opposite: being low in mood may increase their appetite. Food almost becomes an emotional crutch for them.

Irritability

You may find that your child is more irritable than usual. She may lose her temper over seemingly trivial things.

Hopelessness

Your child may feel there is no point to her existence. She may not see a way out of her situation or of how she is feeling.

Guilt

Your child may describe feelings of guilt, but when you explore this with him there doesn't appear to be an explanation for why he feels this way.

Loss of confidence or poor self-esteem

A lack of confidence and problems with self-esteem often go hand in hand with depression. Your child may feel she is not good enough. She may be constantly comparing herself to other people. She may put herself down more than usual. She might pick faults with her physical appearance, saying for instance, 'I am fat, I am ugly.' She may pick holes in her personality: 'I'm so boring, why would anyone want to hang out with me.' It might be that the child lacks confidence when it comes to her ability to do things: 'What's the point in revising? I'm only going to fail anyway.'

We can all be down on ourselves from time to time, but it doesn't automatically mean that we are depressed. However, if your child is consistently down on himself, more than normal, and there are other symptoms of depression at play, then it is worth seeking support from your child's GP.

Loss of libido or lack of interest in sex

This is pertinent if your child is a bit older. It is also something that you would be unlikely to hear about directly from him or her, but it's important to be aware of it all the same. If your son or daughter is in a relationship, it may be the girlfriend or boyfriend who notices that your son or daughter seems less interested in physical contact and in having sex than before.

Unexplained physical health problems

Your child may be complaining of non-specific aches and pains. He may be taking time off school for headaches and tummy pains for which there is no explanation.

Self-harm

When your child is struggling with low mood, she may resort to self-harming as a means of managing her emotions. If your child already self-harms, you may notice an increase in this behaviour when her mood is low. There are different ways your child may choose to self-harm. We will look at these in more detail in Chapter 3.

Table 2 Depression checklist

		Yes	No
1	Is your gut telling you to worry?		
2	Is your child in a low mood? Does he/she seem more tearful than usual?		
3	Is your child lacking energy to do things?		
4	Has your child lost interest in things he/she used to enjoy?		
5	Is your child struggling with his/her concentration?		
6	Does your child seem more withdrawn than normal?		
7	Is your child struggling with his/her sleep?		
8	Have your child's eating habits changed?		
9	Have there been changes to your child's weight?		
10	Does your child seem more irritable than before?		
11	Does your child seem more hopeless than usual?		
12	Does your child feel guilty with no real explanation for it?		
13	Has your child lost confidence?		
14	Is your child being less tactile with his/her partner?		
15	Is your child experiencing problems in his/her relationship?		
16	Does your child always seem to be physically unwell?		
17	Is your child self-harming?		
18	Has your child had thoughts of ending his/her life?		

Suicidal thoughts

Often when your child's mood is very low, she may experience still more negative thoughts. She may question whether there is any point in living. She may experience anything from general suicidal thoughts, where she thinks about not wanting to be alive any more, to more specific thoughts where she considers the ways in which she would take her own life. If your child is very low, she may take this one step further; rather than just experiencing the thought of ending her life, she may actually start planning the detail of how she would go about it. She may even get as far as deciding when and where to act on her thoughts. We will look at suicidal thoughts in more detail in the next chapter.

Dr Vohra's take-home messages: depression

- Think about what your child is normally like. Is her current mood unusual for her?
- Think about what is going on around your child. Is there anything you can see that explains why he may be low in mood? He may have recently broken up with a girlfriend or boyfriend, for instance, or his pet hamster may have died.
- Have a chat with staff at your child's school. Are the teachers worried about your child's behaviour and performance in class?

Traffic light: green

FACE-FEAR

- Have a face-to-face conversation with your child.
- Be attentive; listen to what your child has to say.
- Stay calm.
- Have you run through the depression checklist to get the facts?
- Explain to your child why you are worried.
- Agree an action and, if appropriate, go to amber.

Traffic light: amber

Book an appointment with your GP if you are worried.

Traffic light: red

In case of an emergency, where you are worried that your child is at imminent risk to himself or to others, then contact emergency services or take your child to A&E so he can be assessed by a trained healthcare professional.

3

'I'm worried my child self-harms and is suicidal'

The idea of your child self-harming can be a terrifying prospect for most parents and carers. It can be extremely difficult to broach the topic of self-harm with your child. A lot of parents worry about coming across as judgemental. A natural response for most parents might be 'What did you go and do that for?' Others may find that they become incredibly emotional and upset over self-harming.

There are different forms of self-harm. Let's take a look at the most common.

Self-cutting

Some children may cut themselves using a sharp tool or blade. Children can be quite inventive with what they use. A common trend these days appears to be to unscrew the blade from a pencil sharpener and use this to self-cut. As a parent it is important to ensure, within reason, that your child's immediate environment is safe. If you are concerned about self-cutting, have a think about whether there are any knives, razor blades or sharps at home that are easily accessible to your child. If so, perhaps lock these away.

While such actions may initially help reduce self-cutting behaviour at home, your child may still be readily able to access sharp objects outside the home. Typically some children make use of opportunities to self-harm at school. Your child may borrow scissors from a friend or get hold of a pair that have been used within a lesson.

Why do children self-cut?

It is important to recognize that, more often than not, there will be a reason why your child self-cuts. For many it is a coping mechanism, a way of dealing with the demands and struggles of everyday life. For some, the sight of blood may be what gives them that sense of release or relief. For others, it may be the experience of pain or the actual cutting action that is therapeutic. Children who are depressed may feel numb or emotionless, so cutting may be the one thing that allows them to physically and emotionally feel something.

Overdoses

Non-fatal overdoses – overdoses that don't cause death – may be another way your child chooses to self-harm or self-injure. He may overdose on tablets that are already available within the family home. Things like painkillers (aspirin, paracetamol and ibuprofen) are commonly used by children to overdose. They are cheap and readily available.

Your child may overdose on other medication that is lying around the house, and which belongs to, or is prescribed for, family members. She may root through bedside tables, bathroom cupboards or handbags. Your child may be prescribed medication herself. She may stockpile her own tablets – in other words, not take her medication as

Stockpiling medications

- Ensure that all medication is secured in a lockable drawer or safe.
- If your child is on regular medication, ensure that he takes his medication in front of you.
- If you are unsure whether the child has swallowed the tablet, ask him to open his mouth and say, 'Aah.' This will allow you to have a quick check for any hidden tablets or capsules.
- Is your child able to hold a conversation with you after taking his medication?
- If your child has a headache or is constipated, make sure again that you only give the child the dose that he needs at any one time.
- Try to avoid leaving your child completely responsible for his own medications, particularly if you are concerned about the risk of an overdose.

prescribed, but save it up to take in one go. If you are responsible for giving your child her medication, she may be able to 'pouch' it, that is push it to the side of her mouth rather than swallow it. This allows the child to spit it back out and store it for a later date.

Self-harming is often done in private. You may only find out about it when you catch your child off guard, or at a time of crisis when she can no longer keep a lid on things. It might be that you have caught the child cutting himself or found him following an overdose.

Your child may want to stop self-harming, but may not know how to. For many, up until now, this is what has helped them deal with some difficult emotions. Girls in particular describe being more mindful of their cutting scars during the summer months or when they are getting changed in front of their peers – before and after a PE class, for instance. They may wear loose-fitting, long-sleeve jumpers or tights to cover up scars from self-cutting, even in the sweltering heat. If you do find evidence of self-harm, cuts, bruises or burns on your child, how does the child explain these? Often children who self-harm may give an alternative explanation for their injuries: 'I fell over.', 'I caught myself on some thorns on a rose bush.' Ask yourself if their injuries fit with the explanation they have given.

Other forms of self-harm

- Hair pulling.
- Burning.
- Banging the head.
- Swallowing objects like razor blades and batteries.
- Skin picking.
- Tying objects around the neck, such as a dressing-gown cord or a belt.

Suicidal thoughts

When your child is feeling very low, she may feel that life isn't worth carrying on with and she would be better off dead. The child may find it difficult to open up to friends and family about how bad she is feeling, however close to such people she may be. The child's feelings of distress may come out in other ways. He might be repeatedly self-harming. You may notice that he is becoming increasingly withdrawn. He may even get better at maintaining a front that everything is OK. Getting to the bottom of your child's suicidal thoughts may require you to ask the child outright about them.

Just because a child is feeling worthless and even suicidal, it does not necessarily mean that he plans to do anything about those feelings. A lot of children have such thoughts but are quite clear that they wouldn't act on them. Considering the impact it would have on family and friends is enough to deter them. Nonetheless, the thoughts themselves can be an extremely distressing experience for both you and your child.

Make sure that in such a situation you access support for yourself as well as for your child, because undoubtedly looking after a child who is experiencing thoughts of this nature will have an effect on your own mental well-being.

When a child does decide to end her life, this can either be an impulsive, spur of the moment decision or it may be well thought out. The child may have researched ideas on the internet. It might be that you come across evidence of her planning within her browsing history. She may go to extremes to avoid any chance of being discovered, perhaps making sure that the house is empty or finding a remote location. He may switch off his phone to avoid any chance of being contacted and subsequently disturbed. A situation where a child has gone as far as planning the finer details of what he is going to do and has gone out of his way to prevent family and friends or even a member of the public from discovering him often causes the most concern for professionals, as it reflects the seriousness behind the child's intent.

Ways in which children may take their own life

- Overdose
- Hanging
- Drowning
- Cutting
- Suffocation

What to do if you are worried your child is self-harming?

It can be all too tempting to react to self-harm with anger, upset, disappointment or disbelief. You may try to bargain with your child or beg her to stop. Extreme reactions, and being overly critical or judgemental, often make your child feel worse. She may feel guilty or responsible when all she wants is to feel listened to, understood and supported. It can be useful in these instances to use the mnemonic FACE-FEAR, which was introduced in Chapter 1, to make the conversation around self-harm less fraught.

Be as empathic and understanding as you can and try to remain calm and sympathetic. Show your child that you are emotionally capable of taking on what he tells you. Do not feel guilty about your child's self-harm. As a parent, a natural response is self-blame: 'How did I not notice this was going on? Why was she not able to come and talk to me about how bad things had got?' Don't let this guilt consume you. Instead, focus on showing your child understanding and support.

Finding out more about your child's self-harm
- How long has your child been self-harming for?
- How often has he been doing it?
- Does he self-harm in other ways?
- How does self-harming help the child?
- What are the triggers to the child's self-harm?
- Does the child want help to stop?

Getting your child help for his self-harm

If you are concerned that your child is self-harming, do not hesitate to contact your GP to arrange an assessment. This might be the first you have learned about the child's self-harm, or you may have known about it for some time but are worried that it is happening more frequently. Make sure you explain to your child why you are worried about him or her. It is always important to be open and transparent in your communication.

Make sure, wherever possible, that you include your child in any plans and agree an action together. It may be that you agree to book an appointment with the GP for your child to be reviewed. In circumstances where your child needs a more urgent review,

Table 3 Self-harm and suicidal thoughts or planning checklist

		Yes	No
1	Does your child seem more withdrawn than normal?		
2	Does your child seem to be having more 'accidents' than normal?		
3	Does your child have obvious signs of injury, such as cuts, bruises and burns to his/her body?		
4	Does the injury equate with your child's story?		
5	Is your child wearing long-sleeved tops, even in hot weather, and can't be persuaded to wear anything else?		
6	If your child is known to self-harm, is this happening more frequently than before? Are the child's attempts increasingly risky?		
7	Is your child asking for medication more frequently than usual?		
8	Have you noticed that medication is going missing at home?		
9	Has your child told you about thoughts of not wanting to be alive? Maybe he/she has said this indirectly, such as, 'I wish I could go to sleep and never wake up.'		
10	Has your child posted anything on social media that points to him/her thinking about taking his/her own life?		
11	Have you found anything that could point to the child planning to take his/her own life? Internet browser? Stash of tablets? Unusual items such as rope? Draft suicide notes?		

for example if he or she has an open wound or has taken an overdose of medication, then do not hesitate: contact emergency services or take the child directly to A&E to be assessed.

Following assessment, your child may be referred on to a mental health service provided by the GP or to a specialist mental health service or Child Adolescent Mental Health Service (CAMHS) to assess the child's symptoms further and to look at measures to help with his or her self-harm.

Dr Vohra's take-home messages: self-harm, suicidal thoughts and actions

- Do not blame yourself.
- Remain calm, supportive, understanding and non-judgemental.
- Give your child chances to open up to you about the reasons why she self-harms or why she has thoughts of ending her life.
- If the child doesn't tell you this specifically, ask her directly.
- Take what your child is telling you seriously.
- If you are not the child's parent or carer, but he has confided in you about his thoughts about self-harm and suicide, do not promise to keep the information a secret. If a child is at risk to himself or others, be open and tell him that you have a duty to notify his parents or carers and a professional so that they can access the right support early on.

Traffic light: green

FACE-FEAR

- Have a face-to-face conversation with your child.
- Be attentive; listen to what your child has to say.
- Stay calm.
- Have you run through the self-harm checklist to get the facts?
- Explain why you are worried about your child.
- Agree an action and, if appropriate, go to amber.

Traffic light: amber

Book an appointment with your GP if you are worried that your child may be self-harming.

Traffic light: red

In the case of an emergency, where you are worried that your child is at imminent risk to herself or others, contact the emergency services or take your child to A&E so she can be assessed by a trained health-care professional.

4

'I'm worried my child is anxious'

Amy, 13
Amy has recently moved house and has had to start at a new school. She is someone who struggles with friendships at the best of times and has found adjusting to the new environment hard. Things aren't great at home either and she is struggling to come to terms with her parents' separation. For the last few months, she has found herself waking up in the night in a panic. She can't catch her breath. Her chest feels tight and her heart feels like it is going to jump out of her skin. Her palms feel sweaty and her fingers get a funny tingly feeling in them. It might sound dramatic, but she feels as though she is going to die every time these feelings come on. Things tend to settle down after about ten minutes of her mum trying to calm her down, but Amy ends up feeling exhausted from the whole ordeal. She has started getting these attacks in the day now; anything can set them off. She is constantly waiting in fear that one will come on. She has butterflies in her tummy all the time and she has the idea that something awful is going to happen to her, or to people she cares about.

Her dad tells her she is worrying over nothing and that she ought to pull herself together. If only it was that easy.

We all feel anxious from time to time and your child is no different. Usually there is something to explain our anxiety; maybe it is a stressful event or an unfamiliar environment. For your child, it may be the start of the new school term, exams, a driving test or possibly a new relationship.

Anxiety can sometimes be a valuable emotion for your child to experience. Feeling anxious in the lead-up to an exam, or to a job or university interview, may focus your child's attention and ensure he prepares properly for it. Most of the time anxiety is short-lived, by which we mean it is limited to a particular situation and lasts for a particular period of time before it settles. However, sometimes being anxious is more than just a passing feeling. It may be that it sticks around longer than the person concerned or others would expect it to.

One of the common questions we as doctors are asked is, 'When should I be worried about my child's anxiety?' If your child is experiencing anxiety more often than not, and if it continues for several weeks and even months and is affecting your child's daily functioning, then it is important that you get it checked out.

Triggers of anxiety

Your child may not be able to give you a reason for his anxiety, and it may be that he experiences symptoms without there necessarily being something obvious to set them off.

When your child feels anxious, he may experience symptoms that he can't make sense of. He may ruminate (that is, worry about things over and over again) about the possibility that something bad is going to happen to him or others around him. He may not be able to explain his fears, and there may not be any logic behind them that you can see.

Having time off school can also be an indicator of anxiety, particularly in younger children. Often it can be quite difficult for children to articulate their anxiety, which might show itself in other ways including a run of non-specific physical health problems. You may have taken your child to the GP several times for check-ups for various aches and pains, but these never seem to amount to anything.

Mental or psychological symptoms may be more difficult for parents to pick up than the ones described above. They often rely on your child telling you how and why he is feeling a certain way. It may be that you only get this information by prising it out of the child. There are, however, some subtle signs of anxiety that you may be able to pick up simply by looking at your child. We will run through some of these below. Observing any of these signs may give you some indication that your child is struggling with his emotional or mental health and could give you a starting point for conversations with him.

Physical symptoms of anxiety

Your child may describe some physical symptoms of anxiety. It may feel as if her heart is racing or she has butterflies in her tummy. Her chest may feel tight and she may struggle to catch her breath. She may start to feel sick, or actually be sick. Experiencing these symptoms can be quite frightening, both for your child and for you as a parent watching her go through it.

Some physical symptoms of anxiety may be obvious to you as a parent; for example your child may be trembling or hyperventilating. Other symptoms may be less obvious to the naked eye and may rely on your child telling you about them. The body map in Figure 1 illustrates how certain areas of the body can be affected by anxiety and is a useful reference for children and parents alike.

Mental or psychological symptoms of anxiety

Pacing up and down, restless and finding it difficult to settle It may be that your child is showing signs of physical anxiety. Often pacing can be a way of channelling that anxiety.

Constantly fretting about things Sometimes parents and carers will describe their child getting anxious over something trivial. It is important to be sensitive, show understanding and support for your child. It was probably not very helpful for Amy's father to tell her to 'pull herself together', but such reactions often reflect how frustrated parents feel when they are faced with a child who is unable to articulate her difficulties. As a parent you end up feeling a little helpless and at a loss as to how to move forward.

Twitchier than normal and quick to jump down your throat Being snappy and irritable can often be a sign that someone is stressed or anxious. Obviously, as your child gets older and begins to exert more independence she may become more argumentative

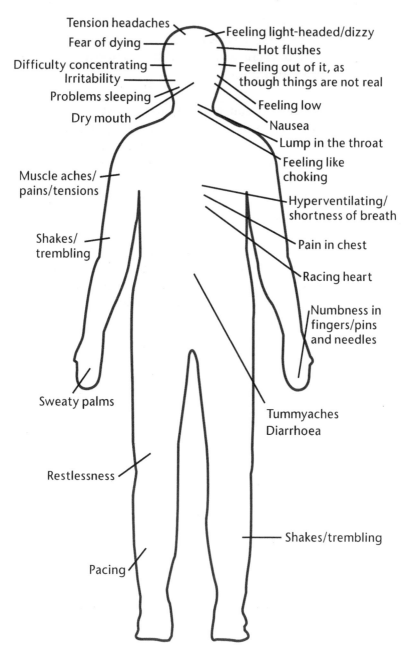

Figure 1 Body map – physical effects of anxiety

and confrontational. If, however, you have noticed that she is consistently irritable without any clear triggers, and that this behaviour is completely out of character for her, then it is worth considering whether there is something else going on.

Finding it difficult to concentrate You may notice that your child seems more forgetful and you are having to repeat things to him more often. Again, this can often be part and parcel of those joyous teenage years, especially if you are trying to rope your child into doing some household chores. But if your child seems to struggle with his concentration most of the time, this can often be an indicator of anxiety.

How is the child's sleep? Your child may find that his anxiety is worse at night when he is less distracted and is left alone with his racing thoughts. He may start to over-think things that have gone on that day. He may struggle to unwind and settle off to sleep as a result of this. Difficulties getting off to sleep, waking up in the night in a panic and waking early in the morning are all common sleep problems resulting from anxiety.

Is your child tired? Feeling tired often goes hand in hand with getting little or no sleep. Your child may feel physically exhausted due to being up for most of the night worrying. It might be that she feels emotionally drained from some of the other symptoms she is experiencing.

Does your child appear down or upset? Not uncommonly, a child may feel low as well as feeling anxious. He may be more tearful than normal. He may feel frustrated with both the emotional turmoil and the physical symptoms that go hand in hand with anxiety.

Anxiety: a vicious cycle

When your child experiences physical symptoms of anxiety, this can sometimes trigger a vicious cycle that ends up reinforcing the anxiety and making it worse. For instance, the child, already feeling anxious, may start to experience shortness of breath or tingling in her fingers and toes, and may feel that her heart is about to jump out of her chest. These physical symptoms can make the child panic, fearing that something is seriously the matter with her. This can make the child feel more anxious, which in turn makes her physical symptoms worse. It is really important when treating anxiety (with support from a qualified healthcare professional) that you help your child to understand the possible triggers of her anxiety (if there are any).

Other forms of anxiety

We have spoken briefly about general anxiety, but anxiety to a healthcare professional is a broad term that covers a whole host of other conditions. This can include things such as social phobia, agoraphobia (a fear of crowded places), panic attacks and specific phobias.

We will cover these conditions briefly, as it is important to recognize just some of the different ways that anxiety can manifest in your child.

Panic attacks

You might have heard the words 'panic attack' tossed casually into everyday conversation. Some people use them to describe an occasion when they felt really anxious and couldn't catch their breath. True panic attacks can be incredibly frightening and disabling experiences. What makes them even more so is when they happen time and time again, and your child can't predict when the next one will come on. It is not unusual for your child to want to avoid certain situations or places that he believes bring on panic attacks. Things may get so bad that the child struggles to leave the house. This might mean, if your child is of school age, that he misses huge chunks of the school term. He may even find it difficult to go out socially with friends and family.

Your child may describe being unable to breathe, his chest hurting, or feeling sick; he may actually be sick. He may feel dizzy or lightheaded or feel a tingling in his fingers and toes. He may feel that everything around him isn't real. He may try to calm himself down but fail, and this can make the panic symptoms worse. He may take himself off to a quiet space to try breathing exercises, or he may rely on someone around him to help bring him out of the episode. Panic attacks do settle eventually, but even the five to ten minutes that an attack lasts can feel like an eternity for your child.

Agoraphobia

This word literally translates as 'fear of the marketplace', but put simply, it is a fear of crowded spaces. If your child has symptoms of agoraphobia she may find it difficult to be in busy places where there are likely to be lots of people. She may make excuses why she can't go out. Perhaps she used to love going to the cinema, shopping with friends or going to gigs, but recently seems less interested or more anxious about the prospect of taking part in these activities.

If your child repeatedly avoids certain places with no particular reason, this might indicate some level of anxiety. When out in public, he may visibly appear anxious, or may make excuses why he has to leave all of a sudden.

Social phobia

Social phobia describes when your child has an overwhelming worry that other people will criticize him. He may avoid certain situations where he thinks this is more likely to happen. Your child may have been asked to give a presentation in front of the whole class and may be extremely anxious about it. The idea of giving a presentation fills most of us with dread, but we would accept the nerves that go along with it and get on and do it. For a child with social phobia, however, the fear can be so disabling that it leads to avoidance of the situation altogether.

Specific phobias

We all experience fears in life, and this is no different for your child. For instance, your child may have a fear of getting on a plane or having a blood test at the doctor's, although with some reassurance she will still be able to get on and do these without it affecting her daily functioning. When your child has a true phobia, she experiences an intense, irrational fear of something. Examples of phobias include a fear of particular animals or insects, heights, or even a trip to the dentist. The anxiety can be so overwhelming for your child that it disrupts her day-to-day routine. She may go to extremes to avoid coming face to face with the feared object.

Your child doesn't necessarily have to come into direct contact with the cause of her phobia. Often just talking about or being shown a photo of the object she fears can be enough to trigger extreme anxiety symptoms or even a panic attack.

Table 4 Anxiety checklist

		Yes	No
1	Has your child told you that he/she feels anxious?		
2	Does your child panic about very trivial things?		
3	Is your child worried that something bad is going to happen?		
4	Has there been a change in your child's mood?		
5	Does your child seem more irritable than usual?		
6	Have you noticed that your child avoids going to certain places?		
7	Have you caught your child pacing up and down?		
8	Is your child going to the toilet more often than usual?		
9	Has your child been physically unwell a lot recently with no real explanation for it?		
10	Does your child tremble or get the shakes?		
11	Has your child told you that his/her heart is beating fast, as if it's going to burst out of his/her chest?		
12	Does your child struggle to catch his/her breath?		
13	Is your child finding it difficult to concentrate?		
14	Is your child having problems with sleep?		
15	Does your child break into a sweat?		
16	Does your child get tingling in his/her fingers?		

Dr Vohra's take-home messages: anxiety

- Your child's anxiety may show itself in physical signs such as shaking or hyperventilating. This chapter's body map will help you pick out the most common of these.
- There may be an identifiable cause for your child's anxiety, as is the case with specific phobias; at other times, there may not be an obvious trigger for your child's anxiety.

Traffic light: green

FACE-FEAR

- Have a face-to-face conversation with your child.
- Be attentive; listen to what your child has to say.
- Stay calm.
- Have you run through the anxiety checklist to get the facts?
- Explain to your child why you are worried.
- Agree an action and, if appropriate, go to amber.

Traffic light: amber

Book an appointment with your GP if you are worried your child is experiencing any of the symptoms of anxiety described in this chapter.

Traffic light: red

Sometimes your child's symptoms may mean that he has thoughts of hurting himself or other people. He may have actually acted on these thoughts and self-harmed, or - if he is known to self-harm - you may have noticed that there is an increase in his self-harming behaviour. If this is the case, you need to access support promptly. Take your child to A&E or contact emergency services so that he can be assessed by a trained healthcare professional.

5

'I'm worried my child has OCD'

Dylan, 10

Dylan is a straight A student. His mum describes him as being super-organized and very particular, even from a very young age. She remembers him colour-coding his toy cars and lining them up in a certain way before playing with them. She didn't think anything of it at the time and just assumed it was a normal thing to do at that age. As he's got older, she has noticed that he will only ever play with three of his cars at any one time; the others have to remain in the toy box. Once he finishes playing with those, he will put them back before getting another three cars out to play with.

When his brother Max plays with him, Max always tips the whole box out on to the floor. Every time he does this, Dylan's heart races, he feels sick to his stomach and he worries that something bad will happen to him if he doesn't immediately tidy them all away. He has to stop what he is doing, go through all his cars again and sort them by colour before he can carry on playing. Only once he has done all that does he feel calmer, but it only takes his brother tipping them out again for the whole cycle to repeat itself. He refuses to have friends round. It only stresses him out having all his cars scattered across the floor.

He is starting to struggle a bit at school. He is handing his work in late and homework seems to take for ever or doesn't get completed at all. He is worried that something bad will happen to his mum if he doesn't check his work three times over. It doesn't help that his brother keeps barging into his room and interrupting him mid-check. When he gets disturbed, he has to start the whole process again. He knows none of it makes sense but he can't seem to resist checking; anything to ease his anxiety.

Obsessive compulsive disorder, or OCD, is a term that we often use in our vernacular to describe people who are excessively organized or 'funny' about how things are arranged, ordered or cleaned. It can be easy to forget that OCD is, in fact, a serious mental illness that could potentially cause your child great distress. True OCD can affect your child's daily functioning, from her relationships with family and friends to how she performs at school.

It may not be immediately obvious to you as a parent that there is a problem. Your child repeatedly checking his work could be mistaken for diligence. It is only when you see the child becoming visibly distressed and made anxious by the whole process that you may wonder if there is something else going on. For instance, Dylan experiences thoughts every minute of every day telling him that something bad is going to happen to him or his mum unless he carries out tasks in multiples of three. When he tries to ignore the thought, his anxiety ramps up. In order to stop feeling anxious, he gives in to the thought and will submit to doing things such as checking his work or playing with his cars in multiples of three. If he is interrupted, he has to start the whole process again; on one occasion he read over the same sentence 12 times just to make sure it was right. It is no surprise that he is starting to hand work in late.

Your child will find the symptoms of OCD incredibly difficult to ignore. She may realize that the thoughts don't make any sense and are irrational, but nonetheless she is unable to stop herself from carrying out her rituals.

Your child's thinking is just one of the things that can be affected in OCD. In the rest of the chapter, we'll consider other signs to look out for should you be worried your child has OCD.

What are obsessions?

The word 'obsession' is used to describe the things that pop into your child's head that ultimately make him feel anxious. These could be thoughts, images, doubts (as to whether the child has or hasn't done something) or urges. Your child may also ruminate, by which we mean he repeatedly goes over things in his mind and worries that something bad is going to happen to him or to his loved ones. Your child will often know that his thinking is irrational or illogical, but this doesn't stop him feeling anxious and distressed about it all the same. In order to stop feeling this way and get rid of the obsession (whether it is a thought, an image or a worry), your child might try to do something to counteract it, or something that he believes will stop the obsession or the bad thing from happening. This is where compulsions come in, and we will look at those later on in the chapter.

Types of obsession

Thoughts

Some examples of thoughts your child may experience include the fear that something is contaminated or that she will get ill, contract a serious illness or die. Your child may also be preoccupied with the idea that something bad is going to happen to her or a loved one. She may even have distressing thoughts of wanting to hurt others.

Images

As well as thoughts, your child's obsessions may come in the form of images or pictures. Your child may describe distressing images that pop into her head. These can include images of destruction, dying or death. They may be images that relate to the child herself, or to her loved ones or the general public. They may even be images that depict the child harming others.

Doubts

Even as adults we experience doubts as a normal part of day-to-day life. Have we turned off our hair straighteners, did we unplug the iron, have we locked the front door? This isn't any different for your child. When we doubt whether we have done something, we normally go back and check it once or twice, even a third time. However, in true OCD, the doubts completely take over and can stop your child from getting on with his daily life; it can affect his social life, his relationships with family and friends, and interfere with school or college. It can be incredibly distressing for the child.

Compulsions

Your child may experience obsessive thoughts, images or doubts in isolation - in other words on their own - or it might be that the obsessions force the child to carry out particular rituals or behaviours to stop him feeling anxious about those thoughts. For example, if your child is fearful of catching a life-threatening illness, he may spend several hours a day washing his hands and showering. In this example, the handwashing and showering is what we call the ritual, behaviour or compulsion; the idea is that washing your hands or showering will undo or cancel out the chance of contracting a serious illness. What we tend to find is that while the handwashing or showering may help in the short term, your child often will have to repeat the actions over and over again to have the same effect. This can obviously be extremely distressing, both to your child who is experiencing it and to you as a parent or carer watching him go through it.

Your child may find that initially she can fit her compulsions and rituals in and around her everyday life, so they might not be immediately obvious to the child's family, friends or school that there is even an issue. It might be that your child confides in you about her difficulties. Often children feel embarrassed or ashamed of their symptoms.

Managing compulsions

Avoid buying in to your child's compulsions to 'reassure him'. For instance, some parents might feel it is useful to check locks themselves to show their child that a door or window is locked and that nothing bad will happen. While it is easy to see why this would be helpful, sometimes it can feed your child's anxiety and – by the very fact you have had to check it too – reinforce the idea that there is reason to be worried about whatever it is feared will happen. Plus, it might mean that your child relies on you for that reassurance, rather than trying to develop it for himself.

Compulsions tend to be fairly time-consuming. Carrying out the ritual once is often not enough to settle your child's anxieties. If your child is interrupted mid-ritual, she may have to start the whole process again. For example, if your child has a compulsion to wash her hands a certain number of times and, while washing her hands, touches the edge of the 'dirty' sink, she is likely to start the whole handwashing process again. This can make the child feel distressed and anxious, particularly if she is up against time constraints. Your child may be able to tell herself that carrying out the compulsion or behaviour is irrational or that it doesn't make sense, but she just can't seem to stop herself doing it.

Routines v. compulsions

It is possible for your child to have normal rituals or behaviours that don't get in the way of his life from day to day but are just things he 'has to do'. Your child may have a lucky number. He may have a particular routine around bedtime which he has to stick to. What sets these 'everyday routines' apart from OCD is how much they impact on your child's family, social or school life and also how much distress they cause to your child if he is unable to follow them.

Rituals can affect the whole family. Often parents or carers may feel frustrated with their child, particularly if the child's behaviours are getting in the way of family life. Parents often describe feeling guilty for wishing that their child would just 'snap out of it'. If your child performs her rituals in the morning, for instance, this may delay getting ready for school and out through the front door on time. This impacts on the wider family and may cause the child's siblings to be late for school or college, and you as a parent or carer to be late for work or other commitments.

So far in this chapter, we have considered compulsions such as handwashing and checking behaviours. Now let's take a look at some others.

Checking locks Your child may go back repeatedly to check that doors or windows are locked. He may have to repeat this behaviour a certain number of times or in multiples of a certain number.

Checking plug sockets Your child may repeatedly check that power sockets are turned off. She may have to plug in and unplug appliances a certain number of times to make sure that this is the case.

Checking on people Your child may have an intrusive thought or image that someone she loves will come to harm. As a result, she may continually check on that person's welfare. She may repeatedly ring or text a loved one several times throughout the day. She may become incredibly distressed if she hasn't heard back from that person. It might be that, in the evening, she forces herself to stay awake to ensure that she can check on a parent, carer or loved one who she fears will come to harm.

Cleaning and cleanliness Your child may have a fear of catching germs, contracting a serious illness or worse still dying. This may lead him to compulsively clean himself (handwashing/showering/bathing) or the environment around him. Your child may meticulously check his body or clothes, and even a speck of dirt may trigger repetitive cleaning behaviours.

Counting Your child may experience an obsessive thought that something bad will happen to the world or he or someone he loves will come to harm. As a way of trying to undo this, or stop the 'bad thing' from happening, he may have to count or carry out particular tasks a certain number of times.

Ordering Your child may line things up a certain way or in a particular order. For instance, it might be that your child has to have her belongings arranged symmetrically and anything that is a fraction out of place will cause her a huge amount of distress.

Touching You might have noticed that your child has to touch certain objects in a particular order before being able to leave a room or move on to another task. The child might fear that if she doesn't touch X, Y and Z, in that specific order, something bad will happen to a loved one. If she loses her train of thought and doubts whether she has touched something the correct number of times, she may have to start the whole process over again.

Repeating words and numbers Your child may find that he is having to repeat certain words, numbers or phrases in his head before being able to carry out a task to prevent something bad from happening.

Table 5 OCD checklist

		Yes	No
1	Does your child seem more anxious than usual?		
2	Is your child being overly clean/hygienic, to the point that he/she is running later and later for school each morning or for other commitments? Is he/she spending prolonged time in the toilet or the bathroom?		
3	Have you noticed that your child's belongings always have to be perfectly aligned and his/her bedroom is always immaculate?		
4	In addition to points 2 and 3 above, have you noticed that your child gets excessively distressed and anxious when he/she touches something 'dirty' or when something in his/her room is moved?		
5	Does your child always seem anxious that something bad is going to happen to him/her or to someone he/she cares about?		
6	Is your child worried about catching a serious illness or dying?		
7	Does your child always seem to be checking things, such as locks?		
8	Does your child regularly have to check or count in multiples of a certain number before he/she can carry out the most basic of tasks?		
9	If your child goes to school, college or university, is he/she running late more frequently and not handing work in on time?		
10	Does your child seem to spend a lot of time on his/her own? Does your child have to eat in a separate dining room from other pupils? Does your child find it difficult to share things with other pupils?		
11	Are your child's grades slipping because he/she is feeling anxious or taking time out of lessons to perform the rituals?		

Treatment: what are the options?

There is a range of treatment options for OCD, depending on how severe it is, from watchful waiting to talking therapies, right through to medication. Sometimes it might be necessary for your child to have a combination of a talking therapy and a medication if their OCD is particularly bad.

Dr Vohra's take-home messages: OCD

- If you are worried that your child or a child you know has any of the symptoms described in this chapter, talk to the child.
- As with all your communication, remain calm, listen, be supportive and understanding. Do not judge your child.
- Get your child to tell you about his or her symptoms. How long has it been going on for? Has it got worse or better? Are there triggers for it that the child can see, in other words things that seem to make his or her compulsions or behaviours worse?

Traffic light: green

FACE-FEAR

- Have a face-to-face conversation with your child.
- Be attentive; listen to what your child has to say.
- Stay calm.
- Have you run through the OCD checklist to get the facts?
- Explain to your child why you are worried.
- Agree an action and, if appropriate, go to amber.

Traffic light: amber

Book an appointment with your GP if you are worried your child is experiencing any of the symptoms of OCD described in this chapter.

Traffic light: red

Sometimes your child's symptoms may mean that he has thoughts of hurting himself or other people. He may have actually acted on these thoughts and self-harmed. If he is known to self-harm, you may have noticed that there is an increase in his self-harming behaviour. If this is the case, you need to access support promptly. Take your child to A&E or contact emergency services so that he or she can be assessed by a trained healthcare professional.

6

'I'm worried my child might have bipolar'

Claire, 17

Claire's parents have noticed a real change in her behaviour over the last few months. She went through a patch of being depressed a few years back, after her best friend died in a car accident. She saw her GP and was started on some medication – an antidepressant. This really helped her. Things were going so well that the GP stopped her medication after six months or so. At first, not much changed and she carried on at college as normal. Her mood was generally a lot better. She was going out and seeing friends again, which she hadn't been doing for a long while.

Mum started noticing Claire wasn't quite right around the time of her AS levels. It was more than your average exam nerves. Every now and again, Mum would walk into her room to check how her daughter was getting on. Each time she did she would find Claire pacing frantically from one end of the room to the other. She was always surrounded by reams and reams of paper. She was burning the candle at both ends and didn't seem to be getting much sleep. Oddly though, she seemed to still have lots of energy, constantly flitting from one thing to the next but not really spending long enough on any one task. She was scatty. She always seemed to be half dressed and was never dressed right for the weather. If it was cold and raining outside, you could guarantee that Claire would be in her shorts. Mum told herself that Claire was probably just stressed with her exams and that it would probably all pass.

It didn't. Claire's behaviour seemed to get more and more worrying. She had started smoking, drinking and staying out late. She brought home a different boy each night. She behaved quite inappropriately at times and didn't seem to have much respect for anyone's personal space. She would be all over people she had just met, to the point that they felt uncomfortable. She was always too happy – 'over the top' happy, high, considering she was sleep deprived. However, she was still losing her cool over the littlest of things.

This all went on for about a week. Then all of a sudden, bam, she was back to being low again. It was like a switch had been flicked. She wouldn't come out of her bedroom. She stopped going out to see friends. She went off her food.

The word bipolar can spark a lot of fear in parents, as the condition is often portrayed quite negatively in the media. It is another term that is often used out of context in day-to-day conversation to describe someone who flits from one extreme of mood to another. However, clinical bipolar disorder is actually a serious mental health condition that can affect your child's relationships with family and friends and impact on his or her school, college or working life.

Diagnosis

Often child psychiatrists tend to shy away from making a diagnosis of bipolar disorder in children. That is not to say it doesn't exist, but in order to meet the criteria for diagnosis, your child needs to have experienced a certain number of episodes of a particular type of emotion within a specific time frame; and by the very fact that children are young, it may be too soon for the diagnosis to be confidently made. In addition, there might be some overlap between the symptoms of bipolar and other common mental health conditions in children and young people. Sudden changes in mood and irritability can often be seen for instance in children who are depressed or anxious.

In the next section, we'll have a look at some of the symptoms and signs associated with bipolar. You may look at these and worry that your child has some if not all of them. Some parents may put such things down to normal adolescence and figure it is all part and parcel of growing up. I suppose we can all at times become irritable, overly talkative or impulsive, depending on what situation we are in, but this doesn't automatically mean that we have bipolar. Have a think. Do your child's symptoms persist, rather than come and go? Do they affect her day-to-day life, from relationships with family and friends to her academic and working life?

What does bipolar look like?

Bipolar is literally just that, polar opposites – literally two poles – of mood. That being said, it is more than just a swing from one mood to the other, from a low to a high. Your child may experience what we call manic symptoms or have an excessively happy or inflated mood, one which is more extreme than you would expect of the child at a particular time or in a particular situation. This 'high' can be incredibly disruptive to your child's day-to-day routine. It affects his personal and family relationships and can even impact on his school or work life. Equally your child may experience very low periods. Your child's depressive symptoms will be similar to the sorts of symptoms we covered in Chapter 2. To avoid repetition we will only look at these symptoms again in brief.

There are different types of bipolar disorder. For the purposes of this book, we will only cover the absolute basics and give you the essential information which will prompt you to get further advice from your GP. I don't want to overcomplicate things by going into too much medical detail. This book is intended to help you recognize when you need to ask for help; it's in no way intended to turn you into a budding psychiatrist.

Broadly speaking, then, in order to be labelled as bipolar you need to have experienced at least one manic or hypomanic episode (hypomania is a less severe form of mania). This means that your child could have a diagnosis of bipolar but never experience depressive symptoms or a depressive episode. If your child has bipolar, he may find that in between the episodes of feeling high and on top of the world and feeling low, his mood returns to normal, or to somewhere between the extremes.

Let's talk manic symptoms

Excitability and elevated mood

If your child has a diagnosis of bipolar and is going through a manic phase, you can expect to see him overly excited and happy.

This tends to be an 'over the top' happiness that doesn't quite fit in with the situation he is in, or with other people's behaviour around him. Often parents will describe it as their child being on a high.

Overactivity

You might notice that your child is taking on a lot, or that she never seems to sit still. Sometimes this overactivity can show in the way she talks. You may find that you are struggling to fit a word in edgeways, that your child is talking too much and too fast and doesn't seem to be drawing breath from one sentence to the next.

As always, it is important not to look at a single symptom and jump to the conclusion that your child has bipolar. I'm sure you can think of plenty of times when your child has been running around non-stop, is full of energy and more active than usual. It might be she is overly excited about an upcoming birthday, in which case her excitement is understandable and appropriate.

Overfamiliarity

Often children or young people who are manic may be overly familiar and friendly with people they hardly know. They may say or do things that are inappropriate. They may be particularly hands-on with someone they have just met. It might be that the way they are behaving is completely out of character for them.

Ask yourself, is your child being friendly or too friendly? Does she seem to have lost her inhibitions? You might worry that your child appears oversexualized, or be concerned that how he is behaving isn't appropriate for his age.

Reduced sleep

Poor sleep often goes hand in hand with overactivity. You may notice that your child is staying up until the early hours, constantly flitting from one task to the next at the expense of sleep. You may find that she is functioning on only a couple of hours of shut-eye but despite this still appears to have enough energy to get on with her day the following morning.

Irritability

Irritability can also be an indicator of mania or hypomania. What is your child's mood like? Is he more irritable than usual? Does she lose her temper easily?

Changes of appetite

You may notice that your child's appetite has suddenly increased and she is eating you out of house and home. While this might be the case in the early stages of hypomania and mania, you may find that as her activity increases and she takes on more, food becomes less of a priority and she loses weight.

Self-importance

Have you noticed that your child has an inflated sense of self? Is he advocating his own self-importance? Does she feel that she was put on this earth for a particular reason or to complete a particular mission? These are just a few examples. These grandiose ideas cannot be mistaken. Your child's ideas, if he chooses to share them with you, will definitely sound odd to you and pretty far-fetched.

Reckless behaviour

It may be that your child has suddenly started indulging in more risky behaviour. She might have started experimenting with drugs and alcohol, when this is out of character for her. He may do things without thinking of what the consequences of his actions might be. He may be spending lots of money and getting himself into debt. She may make snap decisions and do things which mean she puts her own safety and that of others at risk. Sometimes children have a real sense that they are invincible or untouchable so attempt or do things they wouldn't ordinarily think of.

Poor concentration

Often children with mania may struggle with their concentration. They may find it difficult to focus on tasks they have been given and flit from one to another without ever being able to complete each one.

Creativity

Your child may describe feeling more creative. This is often the symptom that most people experiencing mania want to hold on to; it is the one that gives them the buzz. They may have lots of ideas going round their head of things they have to do, coming up with new and exciting ideas that they want to share with you that seem impossible or far-fetched.

Taking too much on

You might notice that your child has suddenly taken lots of things on and is burning the candle at both ends.

Clothing

There may be clues of hypomania or mania in how your child dresses. His clothes may seem a lot brighter, a bit more 'out there' than what is expected or appropriate for a particular season or occasion.

Psychotic symptoms

At the severe end of the spectrum, your child may experience what are called psychotic symptoms. We will cover psychosis fully in the next chapter, but in short, psychotic symptoms tend to be unusual experiences that affect your child's thinking processes or how she senses things. Sometimes children who have symptoms of psychosis may not feel in control of their thoughts. They may experience things such as hallucinations, where they perhaps see or hear things that aren't there. Psychotic symptoms can occur when your child is very low in mood, or is experiencing a high.

Let's talk depressive symptoms

We have covered all the depressive symptoms in Chapter 2, but let us remind ourselves of what the symptoms of depression look like.
    Remember those core symptoms.

Low mood You may notice a sudden drop in your child's mood, particularly if he has not long since experienced a manic episode.

Low energy Your child may have gone from being overactive, flitting from one idea to the next, to suddenly not having the energy to get out of bed on a morning or not being able to keep up with activities such as sporting commitments or school work. Again, if your child has not long ago experienced a high, this will be a very noticeable change.

Lack of pleasure Your child may go from enjoying everything and having a real thirst for life to showing no enjoyment in anything, even things that she used to love doing.

Poor sleep This can be a sign of both depression and mania. Your child may have difficulty getting off to sleep or staying asleep. It is important, though, if you are worried about your child's mood, that you don't rely on sleep as the only indicator. Look at sleep in the context of what else is going on.

Changes in appetite You may notice that your child's appetite is poor and he is not eating as much as usual. Or it might be that, as can often be the case in depression, your child seeks comfort from food. Another useful indicator is to look at your child's weight. Has he lost or put on a lot of weight recently?

Family history

Does anyone in the family have bipolar? While it is not a hard and fast rule that your child will get bipolar if someone in the family has it, a family history does increase their chances and it is information that your doctor will want to know about.

Dr Vohra's take-home messages: bipolar

- Remind yourself of the depression checklist given in Chapter 2.
- Look for sudden changes in your child's mood and behaviour.
- Think about the impact these are having on aspects of your child's day-to-day life, such as friendships, family life and school.

Table 6 Bipolar checklist

		Yes	No
1	Does your child seem unusually or inappropriately happy?		
2	Have there been sudden changes in your child's mood?		
3	Is your child taking a lot on? Does your child always seem to be on the go?		
4	Have there been any dramatic changes to your child's weight?		
5	Is your child surviving on very little sleep?		
6	Is your child being quite reckless? Overspending? Promiscuous? Experimenting with drugs and alcohol?		
7	Is your child acting inappropriately or being overly familiar?		
8	Does your child seem to have over-the-top and far-fetched ideas?		
9	Does your child seem more irritable than normal?		
10	Is your child struggling to concentrate?		
11	Does your child appear to be responding to things that aren't there? Hearing voices or seeing things?		

Traffic light: green

FACE-FEAR

- Have a face-to-face conversation with your child.
- Be attentive; listen to what your child has to say.
- Stay calm.
- Have you run through the mania and depression symptoms to get the facts?
- Explain to your child why you are worried.
- Agree an action, and if appropriate go to amber.

Traffic light: amber

Book an appointment with your GP if you are worried your child is experiencing any of the symptoms of mania or depression described in this chapter.

Traffic light: red

Sometimes your child's symptoms may mean that she has thoughts of hurting herself or other people. The child may have actually acted on these thoughts and self-harmed; if the child is known to self-harm, you may have noticed that there is an increase in her self-harming behaviour. The child may also experience voices prompting her to harm herself or to hurt other people. Your child's manic symptoms may mean that she is taking part in risky behaviour. For instance, your child may be experiencing a high and believe that she is capable of flying, which may prompt her to prove this to people by attempting to jump from a height. If either your child's life or someone else's is at risk as a result of the child's behaviour, you need to access support more promptly. Take your child to A&E or contact emergency services so that she can be assessed by a trained healthcare professional.

7

'I'm worried my child might be seeing things'

Daniel, 13

Daniel's parents have noticed recently that he has been quite withdrawn and is not spending as much time as usual with family or friends. He is not looking after himself. Mum has to literally drag him out of bed and bundle him into the shower, otherwise he would be quite happy to go without. His brother Craig too has noticed a change. Daniel hardly talks to him nowadays and, when he does, it's like he can't concentrate on what his brother is saying. He could have sworn he caught Daniel talking to himself the other day.

Daniel has gone right off his food. He only eats food if it is straight out of a packet, otherwise it ends up in a bin or the dog gets it. He has stopped playing with his computer because he is paranoid that people are watching him through it. He can't deal with the TV being on, so he is for ever switching it off, much to the family's annoyance; he flies off the handle with anyone who tells him to pack it in. He is always sitting in his bedroom in the dark, with his blinds drawn and curtains pulled shut. He is worried that people on the streets are spying on him. He has not been sleeping as well as normal. Mum can hear him walking about until the early hours of the morning. He looks exhausted all the time. She is pretty sure he is not taking any drugs, but can't be 100 per cent certain.

'Psychosis' or 'schizophrenia' can be really frightening and startling words for anyone to hear, let alone a parent or carer. There are so many misconceptions about the condition, such as that 'people with schizophrenia have a split mind or split personality'. Individuals with psychosis may also be viewed as being 'dangerous'; certainly the media and the portrayal of schizophrenia in TV and film have had a role to play in this.

Child psychiatrists will, by and large, try to avoid rushing into a diagnosis of schizophrenia in children and young people. It is possible for children, young people and adults alike to have symptoms that look like schizophrenia, only for it to turn out not to be. We often refer to this cluster of symptoms as psychosis or psychotic symptoms.

We will run through some of the more common psychotic symptoms in this chapter. As with all the other chapters in this book, the rundown of symptoms is in no way intended to frighten you, nor is it trying to turn you into a mini-psychiatrist able to diagnose your own child. Instead, what it hopes to do is educate you in recognizing the early warning signs, give you some idea of what might be going on and empower you to seek advice from your child's GP.

Psychotic symptoms

This list is by no means exhaustive, but it will give you a taster of the sorts of symptoms you can expect to see in a child who might be showing signs of psychosis or schizophrenia. These are things your child's GP or psychiatrist may well ask and get your child to open up about, but it is useful to know what they are and what they mean all the same.

Hallucinations
Auditory hallucinations
Your child may tell you he can hear certain noises or voices that no one around him, including yourself, can hear. Children who experience hallucinations may not realize that is what they are until someone calls them out on it. It's not uncommon for parents to say that they hear their child talking to herself when there is no one else in the room.

Sometimes, as doctors, when we meet your child for the first time, we may notice that she is unable to focus within the session and appears to be distracted by something in the room that is not obvious to us or anyone else present. Auditory hallucinations commonly take the form of voices, and hearing voices is often the main symptom people think of when they first hear the term 'schizophrenia'.

Your child may recognize the voice to be that of a man or woman. It might be the voice of someone the child recognizes or it may be completely unfamiliar. Children may hear several voices as opposed to just one and this can be utterly overwhelming for them. Sometimes the voices are so loud that the child cannot hear himself think clearly or the voices get muddled up with his own thoughts. Often we will ask your child *where* he hears the voice. Can he hear the voice inside his head or can he hear it outside his head, coming through his ears? At times, children struggle to pinpoint exactly where the voice is coming from.

What does the voice(s) say?

It might be that the voice is a kind one, a voice that makes your child laugh or simply comments on everything she is doing. Alternatively, it might be a frightening voice that says horrible things and tells her to hurt herself or other people. The voice(s) may talk directly to your child and command her to do certain things. The voice(s) may talk about your child. Often when your child experiences several voices, she may just hear the voices having a conversation among themselves. All of these experiences can be equally distressing for the child.

Is the voice worse at a particular time of day?

Often children will say that the voice is worse when they are on their own or when they are feeling down. This can often be the case last thing at night. There is no hard-and-fast rule, though; generally, children can hear voices at any time. They may hear the voice every day or only once a week - it varies. Have the voices got worse since your child first started hearing them? It might be that, in the last few weeks, the voices have been coming on more often and are more menacing than they were before.

Auditory hallucinations

Don't forget, while I have referred to a voice or voices here, it may not necessarily be a voice or voices that your child hears. Some children will describe hearing sounds instead.

Visual hallucinations

Your child may describe seeing someone or something that you or others cannot see. Common examples children report include seeing shadows in the corner of their eye and finding, on turning their head, that there is no one or nothing there to explain them. Some children may have more intricate visual hallucinations. They may see in front of them a vision of someone they recognize or someone unfamiliar to them. Sometimes children describe seeing the outline of a figure, but with no face. It may not be a person they see at all, but an object or an animal. Whatever it is, this image will appear very real to your child.

Tactile hallucinations

Tactile hallucinations are physical sensations that your child experiences for which there is no explanation. It might be that the child feels something crawling on him or he may feel someone touching him or feel a breath on his skin.

Olfactory hallucinations

Although rare, it is worth being aware of these. Your child may describe smelling something, such as burning rubber, that neither you nor others around you can.

Thoughts

Psychosis or schizophrenia can affect your child's thinking processes. Here are some of the ways in which this may happen.

Thought echo Your child may feel that the thoughts he has in his head are being repeated and spoken out loud immediately after he has thought them.

Thought insertion Your child may feel that someone or something is putting thoughts into his head. He may not recognize the thoughts in his head as his own.

Thought withdrawal Your child may feel that thoughts are being taken away from her head and that she has no control over this.

Thought blocking Your child may feel that her thinking comes to a stop suddenly, causing her to lose her train of thought.

Thought broadcast Your child may feel that other people around him can hear what he is thinking. This might lead him to act suspiciously around others, even people he knows.

Delusions of control

Your child may describe feeling as though his or her body is being controlled by someone, something or an external force. This can be a really frightening experience for your child to go through.

Changes in speech

Have you noticed any changes in the way your child is speaking to you? She may have gone from someone who was always a bit of a chatterbox to not having very much to say at all. If she is talking to you, her speech may not flow as well as it normally does. It might appear stilted or interrupted. She may start talking to you about something only to tail off unexpectedly or come to an immediate, unnatural halt. It might be that what she is saying to you doesn't make a huge amount of sense. Your child may be making up new words and using them in conversation. Sometimes her speech can appear to be all over the place.

What sort of things might your GP or psychiatrist ask about?

Your child's doctor may want to make sure first and foremost that there is no physical health problem to explain your child's symptoms. Often when your child is physically unwell - with a severe infection, for example - this may have some bearing on his mental health, albeit temporarily. When you first go to see your doctor about your child's psychotic symptoms, the doctor may well request some blood tests. Your child may even be sent by the doctor for a head scan to ensure that there is no underlying physical health problem to explain his or her symptoms.

Drug use and hallucinations

You child may experience symptoms such as paranoia and hallucinations if she is under the influence of drugs. Cannabis is a drug that is commonly associated with paranoia, but hallucinogenic drugs such as LSD and magic mushrooms, which have recently come back into favour with children, can also mimic symptoms of psychosis.

What may you notice?

You may only find out about psychotic symptoms such as those described above if your child feels able to open up to you and tell you about them. If you are feeling brave enough, you may ask about some of the more specific symptoms. You may notice your child talking to himself and ask him outright who he is speaking to. Your child may be upfront with you and tell you, or he may shut down and appear guarded, in which case it may be a struggle to get anything out of him thereafter. It might be that the hallucinations are so distracting that your child can't focus on having a conversation with you at all.

Effects of symptoms on your child's day-to-day life

It is important to consider the effects of any psychotic experiences on your child's day-to-day life. Perhaps you used to be a very close-knit family, but recently you have noticed your child withdrawing slightly and barely talking to you all. Maybe she has completely dropped out of her social circles with no obvious reason why. We expect as children grow up that they will fall in and out of friendship groups, but is this a sudden change with no real explanation behind it? Has your child withdrawn completely from all forms of social contact?

Self-care

Is your child struggling to look after himself? You may notice that the child is less interested than usual in his appearance. We all know how image-conscious some children can be, so if your child has gone from constantly preening herself, doing her hair and make-up before school or before work, to scarcely being able even to muster up the energy to have a shower or attend to basic self-care, then this will obviously be a concern to you.

Effects on school or work

Psychotic symptoms can impact hugely on your child's functioning at school, work or college. Teachers are often a good source of information, whether via informal chats about your child's progress or more formal report cards and parents' evenings. Do teachers constantly express concern about your child's behaviour or academic performance? Is your child normally a high achiever who more recently seems to be struggling to make the grade? What is your child's general behaviour like? Have teachers or friends noticed him acting any differently? Perhaps he is not interacting as much with peers or staff, or when he does so his behaviour appears to be odder and more bizarre than usual. It is important to look at your child's behaviour in the context of what other things are going on around him.

Table 7 Psychosis checklist

	Yes	No
1 Have you noticed that your child seems more distracted than normal?		
2 Have you caught your child talking to or looking at things that don't appear to be there?		
3 Does your child seem more paranoid and suspicious to you?		
4 Is your child saying things to you or to others that don't make much sense?		
5 Is your child struggling with friendships, family, school or working life?		
6 Is your child finding it a struggle to look after him-/herself?		
7 Is your child taking any drugs that you are aware of?		

Dr Vohra's take-home messages: psychosis

- Look for changes in your child's mood and behaviour.
- Think about the impact these are having on aspects of your child's day-to-day life, such as friendships, family life and school.

Traffic light: green

FACE-FEAR

- Have a face-to-face conversation with your child.
- Be attentive; listen to what your child has to say.
- Stay calm.
- Have you run through the psychosis checklist to get the facts?
- Explain to your child why you are worried.
- Agree an action and, if appropriate, go to amber.

Traffic light: amber

If you are concerned that your child has any of the symptoms described in this chapter, then make an appointment for him to see your GP for assessment.

Traffic light: red

Sometimes your child's symptoms may mean that he has thoughts of hurting himself or other people. The child may have actually acted on these thoughts and self-harmed; if the child is known to self-harm, you may have noticed an increase in his self-harming behaviour. The child may also experience voices prompting him to harm himself or to hurt other people. If your child is behaving in a way that could result in harm to himself or people around him, you need to access support promptly. Take your child to A&E or contact emergency services so that the child can be assessed by a trained healthcare professional.

8

'I'm worried my child might have an eating disorder'

Erin, 14

Erin has always been self-conscious about her appearance. She constantly compares herself to her friends. She tells herself she is 'not as pretty', 'not as skinny' and that she is the 'token fat friend'. It doesn't help that one of the lads in her year has said as much. Now, with her prom coming up, Erin's thoughts have gone into overdrive . . .

I went shopping with my friend Hannah the other day. She is tiny. She put a size 6 dress on and it was still hanging off her; I couldn't get a size 6 dress over my fat head, let alone fit into it. She's apparently on this slim shake diet. I've looked into it and might give it a go. I'll try anything if it means not having to turn up to prom looking like a beached whale. I'm not sure quite how I would explain that to Mum. She already knows something is up. She keeps telling me I'm 'not eating enough'.

For the last few weeks, I've tried to avoid eating as much as I can get away with, without making it too obvious, of course. We are one of those families that still sit round the table at mealtimes, which makes hiding things a lot harder. I spend most of the time pushing food around my plate to make it look like I've eaten. I find it easier to do with stuff like rice; I just make a bit of a mound on the corner of my plate and pick out the veg to eat. When Mum asks, I just tell her I've had a heavy lunch or that I made myself a sandwich after school. I'm normally home before them all anyway, so they wouldn't know any different. I find it a bit easier to get away with it at school. Even though Mum sends me into school with a packed lunch, I just unwrap the sandwich, chuck it in the bin when I get there and bring the cling film or foil back home with me.

Although I have lost weight, it's not coming off as fast as I would like it to. I'm trying to do more exercise. I already play hockey but I've started to do a bit more exercise at home. I try to squeeze in half an hour of running on the spot before Mum and Dad get in from work. I also do some ab crunches at night. I normally do it on my bedroom floor, but Mum has started to notice my floorboards creaking and she's almost caught me mid-exercise when she has barged in to see what the commotion is about. I've started doing it on my bed instead, just to drown out the noise. I aim for 500 crunches a night. I've lost half a stone in three weeks. I'm weighing myself every morning and every night just to be doubly sure. My school skirt is definitely starting to feel looser; Mum has already had to take it in a couple of times this term.

For today's generation, so heavily influenced by social media, unrealistic, heavily Photoshopped images seem to be the norm and can feed into your child's body-image insecurities. Your children will, without doubt, compare themselves to boys or girls their own age. Your child may be at an age, particularly as she hits puberty, where she becomes more conscious of her appearance and begins to experiment with her diet. What may start out as just 'wanting to lose a few pounds for a prom' may quickly snowball into something more serious.

> It is important to be aware that while eating disorders are more common in girls, boys can experience them too.

Your child may have an idea of a weight he 'would like to be' or a dress size she would like to fit into. Once the child reaches that target, it is not uncommon for the goalposts to shift and for the child to still 'feel fat', and as though she or he has more weight to lose. It might be that the child becomes drastic in his approach to losing weight, particularly if he has hit a wall with his weight loss. He may start to eat in secret or not at all or make excuses around mealtimes for not eating with the family: 'I've eaten already' or 'I don't feel well'. She may cut out whole food groups or, out of the blue, change her diet abruptly, declaring she's turned vegan or doesn't eat certain things. The child may look at other ways to keep her weight down, such as over-exercising, vomiting or abusing laxatives, which can obviously be alarming for parents to discover.

There are various types of eating disorders. The more common ones that you may have heard of include anorexia nervosa and bulimia nervosa. It is these we will focus on in this chapter. The characteristics of anorexia and bulimia can be summarized as follows.

Anorexia nervosa

- The child may feel fat or fear getting fat.
- The child may be restricting what she eats.
- Over-exercising.
- Vomiting or laxative use.
- Losing a lot of weight.
- For girls, no periods.

Bulimia nervosa

With bulimia, you may notice your child goes through cycles of overeating large amounts of food in a short space of time (binge-eating), followed by periods where she eats less or starves, vomits or uses laxatives as a means of controlling her weight. Other indicators include:

- over-exercising
- vomiting or using laxatives
- the child's weight may be normal
- the child may feel fat or fear becoming fat.

Symptom spotting

The following symptoms are commonly seen in young people with eating difficulties. Parents often find it tricky to tell the difference between what may just be a health kick and what may indicate a problem with food that ought to be cause for concern. Many children use the holidays, particularly the summer holidays, as a time to overhaul their eating. They may register at a gym to pass the time or take up a new hobby. They may have an idea of 'reinventing themselves for the new term'.

Ask yourself if this is indeed just a health kick, rather than something to be concerned about. A sudden interest in diet and exercise, particularly around puberty, can be normal and obviously we want to be advocates of a healthy lifestyle. As always, it is important to look at the symptoms in the context of what else is going on rather than focus on one standalone symptom.

Fear of being fat or becoming fat

What often drives children to restrict their eating and/or to overexercise is the thought that they are already fat and the fear that they will become fatter. Your child may not share these thoughts explicitly with you, but there are some signs to look out for that may indicate your child has a preoccupation with his weight and how he looks. It might be that you catch your child constantly checking himself in the mirror, pinching at skin or 'fat rolls' or you may hear him repeatedly tell you or others that he is fat. As a parent, you may expect to see some of these behaviours during puberty, a time when your child becomes more aware of her body and the changes it is going through. Your child may hold very strong beliefs that she is overweight when it is abundantly clear that she is anything but. However, no amount of convincing will make the child see otherwise.

Avoiding fatty foods or faddy dieting

Your child may have been a very good eater in the past. She might have had the odd dislike, but on the whole you could put most things in front of her and be fairly confident she would polish it off and ask for seconds. Your child's food avoidance may not be obvious straight away. She may start off subtly, leaving the odd scrap of food on her plate. It might be that the child seems to spend longer pushing food around her plate than eating it. This can sometimes give the impression that she is eating, especially if she pushes food to one side or arranges it to look as if she has taken a mouthful here and there. Some children may declare sudden changes to their diet: 'I want to be vegan' or 'I don't want to eat carbs or anything fatty any more.' The food group they cut out might make up the majority of what they used to eat, in which case you would expect them to end up losing a lot of weight in a short space of time. For instance, if your child is normally a carb fiend who would have toast and cereal for breakfast, sandwiches and crisps for lunch and a hearty family meal at teatime, cutting carbs out completely will obviously have a dramatic impact on his weight.

Preparing their own food

Carbohydrates ('carbs') and fats tend to be the food groups that your child is most likely to avoid. On top of this, your child may track the calories contained in the food and drink that she is taking in. You may notice that your child suddenly has a preference as to how things are prepared or cooked. He may refuse to eat what the rest of the family is eating because he perceives it to be 'too fatty', 'too oily' or 'too unhealthy'. Your child may insist on preparing her own food and eating something separate from the rest of the family.

Skipping meals

You may notice that your child has begun skipping meals. At weekends and during school holidays, it may be easier to monitor what he eats each day, particularly as you are around him for longer periods of time. During the school term, however, your child spends a huge chunk of time away from home and you may not be so aware of what he is eating or whether the lunch you prepared for him to take to school has been eaten or not. You may be giving your child money for lunch, in which case there is an added level of uncertainty about what he is eating, if anything at all. It is not uncommon for children who take a packed lunch to empty the contents out at school so it appears that they have eaten it.

Teachers and other staff at school may notice that your child isn't coming into the hall for lunch. It might be that her friends have noticed that she doesn't join them for break times or lunch and that she is always making excuses not to be around food.

You may notice that when it comes to family mealtimes, your child is making excuses for not sitting down and joining the family at the table: 'I ate something earlier' . . . 'I'm not hungry' . . . 'I don't feel well.' These can all of course be legitimate reasons for someone not to want to eat, but if for instance it ends up with dramatic weight loss and, in the case of teenage girls, no longer having periods, then you may reasonably assume that your child is struggling with eating.

Eating out

This can be an overwhelming obstacle for a child who is in the grip of an eating disorder. Eating out has become as much about the socializing as it has the eating. Your child may refuse to go out for a meal with family or friends. If he does manage to come along, he may seem hugely indecisive about what to order or pick around the food on his plate when it arrives. He might be overly interested in how it was prepared and opt for the blandest or least calorific option on the menu.

Preoccupation with food

Your child may still appear on the surface to take an interest in food, in the sense that she will prepare it, cook it and serve it to other people. One thing to bear in mind, particularly if you are worried about your child's weight, is that this enables her to have some control over the ingredients used, such as the amount of fat and so forth. It is also easy to make the assumption that because your child has made it, she will eat it. It might be that your child excuses herself from eating with the family because 'I've been grazing as I've been cooking and I'm too full up.'

Weight loss

The most obvious indicator of an eating difficulty or disorder is weight loss. Saying that, your child may go to real efforts to hide the problem. She may wear several layers of clothing or wear baggy clothes to hide her weight loss. This makes spotting the signs all the more tricky. It can be difficult for parents or carers to monitor their child's body shape or size, particularly as children get older and become more independent. For instance, it would be rare for a parent to help their child in getting ready for school, in terms of washing or dressing the child, especially once she reaches a certain age. As a parent or carer, it may not be until the weather is warmer, when your child naturally may wear less clothing, that you first get a glimpse or a sense of her weight loss.

Holidays, particularly in sunnier climes, have proved to be a common place for parents or carers to come face to face with the stark reality of an eating disorder. For many, that may be the first time for many months they have seen their child in a swimming costume. It may be harder for your child to hide what is going on in the blistering heat. Saying that, if your child insists on wearing multiple layers of clothing even in the heat, this too might indicate that something is wrong, and it is worth exploring this with your child.

We can gauge weight loss by measuring inches or monitoring weight on the scales. It is likely that your child will have some way herself of keeping track of her weight loss. She may be weighing herself once a day or several times each day, perhaps after every meal. If there aren't any scales in the house, your child may go by how her clothes fit. She may aim to get down to a particular dress size or to fit into a particular item of clothing. Your child can often be quite secretive about what her end goal is, and you may not realize the extent of your child's difficulties until you access appropriate help and she opens up to a healthcare professional.

Over-exercising

Your child may not only control her weight by cutting down on the food she eats but may also over-exercise to counteract whatever calories she is taking in. If your child is usually very active anyway, this may be more difficult to decipher. The child may find different ways of over-exercising, from going to the gym every day to exercising on the spot in her bedroom. It is not uncommon for children to exercise on their bed, maybe doing repeated body-weight exercises to avoid any sudden thuds to the floor that may draw attention to what they are doing. It might be that your child waits until everyone is out of the house before doing her daily exercises.

Taking over-the-counter medications (laxatives or appetite suppressants)

As you are no doubt aware, laxatives and appetite suppressants are readily available to buy, both online and face to face at your local chemist. They may be within easy reach at home. You may notice, if you use them, that you are having to replace them more often than before. Your child may tell you that he is bunged up and ask you to buy him laxatives, only for these to be misused as a means of controlling his weight. If your child regularly asks for laxatives, try to get a sense of whether he is using them legitimately or misusing them. Seek advice from your GP if you are unsure, or if you have concerns. The GP will at the very least be able to ensure that a physical cause is ruled out.

Appetite suppressants

Appetite suppressants are a bit of a minefield. You only need to flick through a magazine, turn on the TV or switch on your computer to see one being advertised. For those readily available and unpoliced on the internet, we have no idea what they are made up of or what harm they can potentially cause to your body. Sometimes this can be the last thing your child is worried about, particularly if she is desperate to get a quick weight-loss fix. Be alert to suspicious packages that come through the door, unusually labelled bottles or tablets or particular concoctions that your child may be taking, and don't be afraid to ask questions.

Vomiting

Your child may intentionally make himself sick as a means of controlling his weight. You may notice your child is making excuses to go to the toilet or bathroom immediately after he has eaten. You may overhear him retching. Perhaps you follow him into the bathroom and smell vomit or the efforts he has made to cover up his tracks, such as overuse of perfume or air freshener. You may smell vomit on his breath. If your child has been vomiting for some time, one of the things that he may develop are calluses (hard skin) on the backs of the fingers where his teeth have rubbed up against them through repeatedly putting his fingers down his throat.

Change in periods

This can often be the most alarming of symptoms for the parents and carers of girls, particularly as it raises all sorts of concerns, not least about your daughter's fertility in later life. When your daughter is underweight, she may never experience a period, or maybe she used to have regular periods which have ground to a

Table 8 Eating disorders checklist

	Yes	No
1 Have you noticed any changes in your child's weight?		
2 Does your child seem more preoccupied with how he/she looks than before? Does the child think he/she is fat?		
3 Does your child seem to have low self-esteem and lack body confidence?		
4 Do you have concerns that your child is repeatedly weighing him-/herself?		
5 Have there been any sudden changes to your child's diet?		
6 Is your child making excuses why he/she can't sit with the family at mealtimes or go for meals out?		
7 Does your child spend longer playing with his/her food than eating it?		
8 Does your child seem a lot more interested in how his/her food was cooked than usual? Does the child seem focused on counting calories?		
9 Has your child started to prepare or ask for different meals from the rest of the family?		
10 Are you worried that your child might be over-exercising?		
11 Does your child always disappear to the toilet or bathroom after a meal?		
12 Can you see any evidence of your child having vomited? Traces in the toilet bowl, lingering smells or the sound of retching?		
13 Are there lots of hidden food wrappers? This may be evidence of a binge.		
14 Do you suspect that your child is using laxatives or appetite suppressants?		
15 If your child is a girl, have her periods stopped or did her periods ever start?		

▶

Table 8 continued

16	Does your child have calluses on the backs of his/her fingers?		
17	Have there been changes to your child's mood recently?		
18	Has your child been physically unwell recently? Does he/she often feel light-headed and dizzy?		

halt since she lost weight. This is a worrying sign, as it is her body's way of saying that it is not getting the nourishment that it needs to perform this basic function.

Dr Vohra's take-home messages: eating disorders

- Eating disorders can be highly secretive illnesses.
- Your child will likely not see that there is a problem with her eating and will still believe she is fat.
- It is often down to you as the parent or concerned adult to seek support for your child on her behalf.

Traffic light: green

- Have a face-to-face conversation with your child.
- Be attentive, listen to what your child has to say.
- Stay calm.
- Have you run through the eating disorders checklist to get the facts?
- Explain to your child why you are worried.
- Agree an action and, if appropriate, go to amber.

Traffic light: amber

If you are concerned about your child's lack of appetite and weight, then book him or her in to see your GP for an assessment. It is likely in the first instance that the GP will examine the child physically, give her some blood tests and get a tracing of her heart to measure the impact on the child's physical health.

Traffic light: red

Often children with eating disorders struggle with their mood. Sometimes your child's symptoms may mean that she has thoughts of hurting herself or other people. She may have actually acted on these thoughts and self-harmed; if she is known to self-harm, you may have noticed that there is an increase in the child's self-harming behaviour. Your child may also describe thoughts about no longer wanting to live. Your child's physical health may have taken a turn for the worse as a result of his or her difficulties. If any of these scenarios present themselves and you are worried that your child's life is at immediate risk, then ensure you seek support promptly. Contact emergency services or take your child to A&E for an urgent assessment.

9

'I'm worried my child might have ADHD'

John, 8

John is constantly getting into trouble at school. He plays up in class, distracts his friends, laughs at the teacher and answers back. He is falling behind in almost every subject. When his teacher asks him to do something, it goes in one ear and out the other.

It is no different at home; his concentration is awful. There have been a few times where he's been out with Mum and he's not bothered to look where he is going, almost getting himself run over in the process. He is impatient and is constantly queue jumping. He always rushes to answer questions that are not meant for him. He has got himself caught up in some sticky situations from not properly thinking things through. He has lots of energy and is always on the go. He never sits still.

Story time at school is no fun for his teacher, who seems to spend half the time chasing him round the room and telling him to sit down like the rest of the class.

You may have heard of attention deficit hyperactivity disorder or, as it's more commonly known or abbreviated to, ADHD. It is one of those conditions that is often misrepresented by the media. There is an idea that children with ADHD are just 'naughty kids' who can't be controlled by their parents, which is simply not the case.

Parents who have children with ADHD do inevitably feel guilty. They often wonder whether it is down to something they have or haven't done as parents.

In this chapter, we'll take a look at ADHD, help you understand it better and give you the confidence to approach your doctor if you are concerned that your child may have it.

Symptoms of ADHD

There are three main symptoms of ADHD.

1 Your child may find it *difficult to concentrate.*
2 He may have lots of energy, be constantly on the go and gener-ally *hyperactive.*
3 She may be *impulsive,* which means she makes decisions or acts on things before thinking through the consequences.

Your child will experience these symptoms wherever he is, whether at home, in public, at school or at work.

Difficulty concentrating

Children with ADHD often struggle to concentrate and are easily distracted. Your child may start playing up in class or be a trouble-maker. This is often something teachers at school will notice and may reflect back to you at parents' evenings or in your child's re-port card.

At home, you may notice that your child is more forgetful than normal. You may have asked her to do something and find you have to repeat yourself more than once. Your child may end up in risky situations through not concentrating - for instance, not look-ing where he is going when he crosses the road. It can be difficult for parents to work out whether an older child's lack of concen-tration and forgetfulness is simply down to being a teenager. We all know children can be selective in what they listen to, especially when it comes to their parents. Certainly, we expect that, as kids get older and become more independent, they may be less and less interested in what their parents have to say to them, but we would expect a child with ADHD to have struggled with their concen-tration from a very young age, and to have consistently experi-enced problems throughout their childhood.

Hyperactivity

Children with ADHD have lots of energy - more than we would expect in a given situation. Obviously, there will be certain times when kids have boundless energy, such as when they are enjoying

Table 9 ADHD checklist

	Yes	No
1 Is your child always on the go?		
2 Does your child seem to have lots of energy?		
3 Do you find that your child is always like this and is difficult to control in situations where it isn't appropriate?		
4 Is your child fidgety, finding it difficult to sit still?		
5 Do you find that your child is struggling with his/her concentration?		
6 Are you having to repeat things over and over again to your child?		
7 Have your child's teachers or work colleagues commented about his/her lack of concentration?		
8 Is your child doing poorly in his/her school work?		
9 Is your child making mistakes at work?		
10 Does your child struggle to follow instructions?		
11 Has your child found him-/herself in risky situations because he/she has not been concentrating?		
12 Does your child do things without thinking through the consequences?		
13 Does your child constantly push in or jump queues?		
14 Does your child find it difficult to take turns in conversation and constantly interrupt?		
15 Have you noticed this problem for some time throughout his/her childhood?		
16 Is your child's behaviour the same no matter where he/she is or who he/she is with? Have teachers also noticed this?		

the excitement of a party. When we think about hyperactivity in the context of ADHD, your child's level of energy won't be in keeping with or appropriate for that particular situation. You might find, for example, that your child struggles to keep still or always needs to be occupied with some activity or other. She may be restless or always on the go, having to be constantly active. At school, she may find it difficult to sit still. She may constantly interrupt the class, getting up and pacing around.

Impulsivity

As parents, you may notice that your child says or does things without thinking. He may have no filter and blurt things out in conversation that are inappropriate, so that you constantly have to pull him up on it. He may do things without thinking that could put him at serious physical risk. He may dabble in drugs and alcohol and make snap decisions without thinking through the consequences of what he is doing. Your child may have no real sense of danger.

At school, teachers may notice that your child is constantly interrupting the class by talking too much, without the filter or 'off switch' that you would expect him or her to have in certain social situations.

Dr Vohra's take-home messages: ADHD

- As with all the symptoms we cover in this book, try to avoid looking at one symptom in isolation. If your child is not concentrating, this does not automatically mean she or he has ADHD.
- It is important to look back at your child's early years and ask yourself how long the child has experienced such symptoms. Is she struggling in these ways regardless of where she is, whether at home, with friends or at school?
- Hyperactivity, being impulsive and lack of concentration are all signs of ADHD. Children who experience one or all of these symptoms will be affected in all areas of their life, from their ability to hold down a friendship to their school life.

Traffic light: green

FACE-FEAR

- Have a face-to-face conversation with your child.
- Be attentive; listen to what your child has to say.
- Stay calm.
- Have you run through the ADHD checklist to get the facts?
- Explain to your child why you are worried.
- Agree an action and, if appropriate, go to amber.

Traffic light: amber

If you are concerned that your child may have signs of ADHD, it is important to book an appointment with your GP so this can be properly assessed.

Traffic light: red

If your child is impulsive, doing things without thinking through the consequences and putting herself or others at imminent risk of harm in the process, then make sure that you contact emergency services or take the child to A&E.

10

'I'm worried my child might have autism'

Joe, 11
Joe's mum has always worried that he was different from all the other kids his age. He wasn't the easiest of babies. He hated being held, for a start, and would take ages to settle. He has always been a fussy eater and there are certain foods he doesn't like the feel of. He was and is still obsessed with beige foods: bread and potatoes are his staples and if his mum gives him anything different, it stresses him out no end. She is for ever preparing him something separate from the whole family. Eating out as a family is almost impossible.

He went to nursery from a young age, but really struggled to get on with the other children, preferring his own company to anyone else's. If he did play with the other kids, it would always be on his terms. He struggled with his speech when he was younger and was late talking. He has always found school quite difficult, particularly the need to interact with people day in, day out. He can barely look anyone in the eye, even when they are talking to him. He has made a couple of friends, but they just spend their time playing computer games next to one another rather than talking about anything deep and meaningful.

Autism

The three main symptoms of autism are as follows.

1 Difficulties communicating - that is, your child's language skills.
2 Difficulties with social interactions.
3 Having very specific interests or repeating certain behaviours.

Your child may find it difficult to interact socially with kids her own age and there may be certain rituals and behaviours that she has to stick to. She may continue to struggle with her verbal communication and as a result fall behind academically. Conversely, some children with autism have a high level of functioning in certain areas, to the extent that they perform on a par with or even exceed their peers. They may seem formal and adult-like in their language.

Let's now look at the main characteristics of autism in more detail.

Communication difficulties

Children with a diagnosis of autism often have difficulties with their communication skills. It may be that they were late beginning to talk and may have continued to struggle with speech as they have grown older. Their speech might be limited. You may have noticed problems not only with what they say but also how they say it. They may behave unusually as they are talking to you - their non-verbal communication, such as their gestures or eye contact. From a young age, parents may notice that their child didn't smile or wasn't able to make eye contact - or if the child did, he would find this very difficult.

Social interaction

The nursery staff have noticed that your child wasn't joining in with group activities and preferred to play on her own. Some children with autism will find it difficult to share tasks or enjoyment with other kids. Mums may have noticed that their child wouldn't interact with the other kids on play-dates, that he would be happy enough playing on his own, or if he did play with other kids it would be on his own terms and according to his rules. You may find that your child has difficulty understanding things from other people's perspective. Your child may struggle to put himself in other people's shoes and think about how others may be feeling in certain situations. Your child may struggle to understand subtleties in conversation. She may find it difficult to strike a balance and to make conversation a two-way thing. She may show little interest in what the other person has to say, so any conversation ends up feeling a little one-sided. Often children with autism will take things very literally, so your child may find it difficult for example to pick up on sarcasm.

Special interests

You may find that your child has very specific or unusual interests. He may be good at remembering particular dates. He may be fascinated by the wheels on a bicycle, or by each individual spoke. The child may spend his time reading up on these interests and studying them closely. Your child's interest in these things may be more all-consuming than you would expect the average person to be, and can seem somewhat intense.

Repetitive behaviours

Your child may have certain rituals, behaviours and routines that he sticks to every day. Often children with autism are very particular and rigid with their routines.

Your child may show no flexibility in his usual routine, and any change in this may cause him a lot of anxiety and distress. For instance, it might be that your child is always the first in the shower or first down to breakfast. She may always eat the same amount of cereal out of the same bowl each day. It might be that, one day, her favourite bowl is still being cleaned in the dishwasher and, as a result, you give her a different one to eat out of that morning. What might seem like a trivial thing to anyone else (not having her normal bowl) can be a source of much anxiety and distress for your child, to the point that she may refuse to eat breakfast altogether.

Plenty of us have particular routines and structures that we like to stick to, but we can be flexible in situations where it may not be possible to do so - in the example above, most of us would simply pick up another bowl. However, this one slip-up can potentially have a real knock-on effect on your child's functioning for the rest of the day.

Repetitive movements

Sometimes children with autism may make unusual movements. For instance, they may repeatedly shake their fingers in a certain way or move their head or feel impelled to rock themselves back and forth. They may also be sensitive to light, sound and textures around them.

Sensory difficulties

Often children with autism may be hypersensitive to certain noises, lights, colours, textures or smells. They may feel overwhelmed when they come into contact with these and this can often trigger 'meltdowns' as a result of an overload of their senses. For instance, they may struggle in crowded spaces where there are lots of people, such as a social gathering or on a train or a bus, or they may struggle at a disco where there are bright flashing lights or other places where there is a lot of noise.

Sometimes children and young people with autism will only wear certain clothes because they don't like the feel of certain textures on their skin. They may stick to the same type of clothing and get highly distressed when it is not available to them. They may need to have the labels cut out of clothing because they don't like the way these feel next to their skin.

Even something as simple as a hug from a close family friend can trigger a meltdown in a child who is hypersensitive to touch.

Don't overthink things

As a parent, when you are waiting at the school gates, it is only natural for you to draw comparisons between your child and his peers. You might notice that some children are louder than others. You may notice some children congregating in groups while others prefer to play on their own.

Although children with autism do tend to struggle with social interaction, this is not to say that every child who plays on his or her own must have autism.

As with any of the symptoms we discuss, just because your child has one symptom do not jump to the conclusion that he or she has autism. If you are concerned, go and see your doctor, who will be able to assess the child and look at her symptoms in the context of what else is going on.

Your doctor will be keen to work out when you first started noticing that your child had difficulties in these areas. If the problems started before the child was three years old, this can make a diagnosis of autism more likely.

Autism in early childhood: what might your doctor want to know?

Your child's GP or doctor will be interested in what the child's development was like, right from birth through to their current age. Every item of information forms an important piece of the jigsaw. Such details may seem trivial to you, but they are hugely important when it comes to considering whether your child has a developmental disorder such as autism. This can often be a bit of a memory test for parents, as they struggle to recall the exact details of what their child was like as a newborn.

This is where your child's red book can come in handy! The 'red book' or personal health record is given to you by the health visitor shortly after your child's birth. It provides an overview of your child's physical health, as well as recording his weight and height and when he reached certain development milestones such as walking and talking. It also includes the dates of various check-ups, periods of illness, routine vaccinations and medications prescribed for your child.

Pregnancy   Your child's doctor will likely want to know everything, right from your pregnancy. Was the pregnancy straightforward? Did you struggle with your physical or mental health? Did you smoke, drink or use any other substances during your pregnancy?

The delivery   Did your child arrive as expected? How many weeks pregnant were you? Did you have a vaginal delivery or did the baby have to be delivered by caesarean? Did your child need any time on a special care baby unit? Were you in and out of hospital fairly quickly or did you and your child need to stay in for a bit longer?

The early days   How did your baby feed? Was he breast or bottle fed? Was she a fussy feeder? Again, be assured that not all this information will necessarily point to a diagnosis, but it allows your doctor to put your child's difficulties into context.

Milestones and feeding Did your child walk and talk when you expected him to? How was potty training? What was your child like with her food? When we speak to parents whose children have a diagnosis of autism, they often describe them as being really fussy with their food. They may be really particular about certain textures of food. For instance, they may prefer to eat puréed food and refuse to eat anything with lumps. They may stick to foods of a certain colour and you might find it a real battle to get them to eat anything else.

The food dilemma

I am sure that, as parents, you face battles almost daily with your children over food and this can be the norm for most kids growing up. 'I don't want to eat this, I don't want to eat that' – it can be difficult to work out how much is down to illness and how much is part and parcel of growing up and developing tastebuds!

Playtime

Your doctor will show a real interest in how your child interacts with other children. Does your child share toys and games with other children and is he able to play with them or does he prefer to play on his own but alongside other children? Your child may have to line up his toys in a particular order or sort them by colour. He may have particular rules that he will expect other children he plays with to follow. He may have certain toys or subjects that he is very interested in and knowledgeable about.

Is your child able to role-play and be imaginative in her play? Does your child play with dolls and re-enact everyday life using her toys? Does she look for inventive ways of using objects for a purpose other than what it is intended for? For example, she may use a cardboard box as a car or a remote control as a telephone. Children with a diagnosis of autism often struggle with role-play or imaginative play. They may also struggle to play with other children, not enjoy the physical play or sport that other children do and prefer their own company.

Table 10 Autism checklist

	Yes	No
1 Does your child struggle to hold conversations with other people?		
2 Has your child always struggled with his/her speech, even from a young age?		
3 Is your child's speech very monotonous?		
4 Does your child find it difficult to make eye contact when talking to people?		
5 Have you noticed any odd movement that your child makes over and over again for which there isn't a clear purpose?		
6 Have you noticed that your child doesn't really use non-verbal means of communication, such as gestures, smiles or other facial expressions?		
7 Does your child find it difficult to read other people's emotions or put him-/herself in other people's shoes?		
8 Does your child seem to spend a lot of time on his/her own and find it difficult to make friends?		
9 Have you noticed these difficulties with your child since below the age of three?		
10 Has anyone in the family received a diagnosis of autism?		
11 Does your child seem to have particular rituals and routines that he/she has to stick to? Does he/she get overly anxious if these are not adhered to?		
12 Does your child have very specific foods that he/she will or won't eat? Only certain clothes and textures that he/she will tolerate wearing?		
13 Does your child find it difficult to enjoy activities that you would expect him/her to at his/her age? Does your child struggle with going to kids' birthday parties or family gatherings?		
14 Does your child struggle to understand sarcasm and take things very literally?		

Dr Vohra's take-home messages: autism

- As with any condition, it is important not to assume that, just because your child has one of the symptoms above, he or she must have autism. It is possible for your child to eat nothing but beige convenience foods and not have a diagnosis of autism.
- Your doctor will look at your child's symptoms in the context of what else is going on and will be interested in his or her development from an early age.
- Your GP might refer your child to a paediatrician or a child psychiatrist to do a thorough structured assessment.

Traffic light: green

FACE-FEAR

- Attempt to have a face-to-face conversation with your child.
- Be attentive; listen to what your child has to say.
- Stay calm.
- Have you run through the autism checklist to get the facts?
- Explain to your child why you are worried.
- Agree an action and, if appropriate, go to amber.

Traffic light: amber

If you are concerned that your child has symptoms of autism, book an appointment with your GP for the child to be assessed.

Traffic light: red

Sometimes your child's symptoms may mean that he or she has thoughts of hurting himself or other people. The child may have actually acted on these thoughts and self-harmed; if he is known to self-harm, you may have noticed an increase in his self-harming behaviour. If you are concerned that your child is at risk of hurting himself or others, then ensure you seek support promptly. Contact emergency services or take your child to A&E for an urgent assessment.

11

'I'm worried my child has PTSD'

Beth, 9
Beth was involved in a car accident last year. Her friend Jamie's mum was driving. Beth and Jamie were sitting in the back. Beth had to go to hospital for a few cuts and grazes but luckily she didn't need to be admitted. It was fortunate that no one was seriously hurt. Since the accident, however, Beth has found it difficult to get into a car without breaking into a sweat. She panics. Her heart pounds right out of her chest, she suddenly starts breathing faster and panics that she is going to suffocate. She has started walking to school rather than getting a lift from her parents; luckily they don't live too far away. She keeps having flashbacks to the accident and relives it in her mind. These flashbacks feel so real. She can smell the burning rubber of the tyres and can almost hear the rain that was falling on the night it happened. She hasn't been sleeping well. She wakes up in a panic, unable to catch her breath. Every night she worries about going to sleep because she's afraid she will have another nightmare.

We can all be shaken up or left reeling when something terrible has happened to us. It might be that we feel anxious, on edge, for a little while after the event. We may avoid going to certain places that remind us of what has happened. But in time we are able to get back to normal without needing professional help or support. In cases of post-traumatic stress disorder - or PTSD, as it is more commonly referred to - this process is less straightforward. Most people will have heard of PTSD in the context of war. Soldiers return home after serving their country, having witnessed unimaginable scenes and, as a result, are hugely traumatized. PTSD can occur as a result of a number of events, however, and can affect anyone, at any age.

What might trigger PTSD?

Triggers for PTSD range from being involved in a car accident to witnessing a terrorist attack. Often the young people I see who have symptoms of PTSD may have been the victims of abuse in their past, whether emotional abuse, physical abuse, neglect or sexual abuse.

Your child may not necessarily develop symptoms of PTSD immediately after the traumatic event. It may take days, weeks, months or in some cases many years before he shows signs of being affected. When your child does develop symptoms, it can have a huge impact on his day-to-day life. He may struggle with going to school, or it might affect his relationships with friends or family.

Symptoms of PTSD

Reliving what has happened

Your child may experience flashbacks of the traumatic event. She might have these flashbacks in the daytime or at night, when they can take the form of nightmares which stop the child from getting to sleep. These can happen over and over again, every day or every night. The flashbacks and nightmares are extremely vivid and can feel as real as the event itself to the child experiencing them. Even certain smells, textures or materials can be enough to trigger a memory.

Physical symptoms

Your child may also experience physical symptoms of anxiety, which may be easier for you to spot. The child may be shaky or break out into a sweat. He may hyperventilate and find it a struggle to catch his breath. Your child may feel like his heart is going to jump out of his chest. Some children even experience pains in their chest. Sometimes when children are anxious they can feel lightheaded, as if they are going to pass out; they may even end up doing so.

You may have noticed that your child's sleep is all over the place. She may tell you that she is having nightmares. You might find that your child is waking up more frequently and is generally more difficult to settle. He may have started wetting the bed again.

Avoidance

During the day, you might notice that your child is more withdrawn than normal. She might avoid certain situations that remind her of what has happened. Say, for instance, that your child has started developing symptoms of PTSD following a car accident: she may be unable to get into a car, preferring to walk everywhere. Even the thought of getting into a car may be too much for her, and she may start to feel panicky or anxious. This can trigger flashbacks that bring the child back to the traumatic event.

Other symptoms

Difficulty concentrating When children experience anxiety or symptoms of PTSD they find it difficult to concentrate. They may seem more distracted than normal. The school may notice that their grades are slipping. Parents may notice that their child is more forgetful and is having to be reminded to do things more than usual.

Changes in mood and behaviour You might find that your child is low in mood or more tearful than normal. It might be that he feels numb or cut off from his emotions. She may seem more irritable. She may experience outbursts of anger. He may lose interest in activities that he used to enjoy and make excuses for why he can't join in. Your child may find it difficult to relax. She may constantly be on edge or on her guard for danger.

> *Depression and anxiety: a recap*
>
> Look back at Chapters 2 and 3 to remind yourself what signs to look out for if you are concerned that your child is presenting as low in mood or anxious.

Time off school Your child, and particularly younger children, may not necessarily be able to communicate to you how they are feeling. Instead, this may be expressed through physical symptoms. The child may be taking time off school because of various physical complaints, such as non-specific tummy pains or feeling sick. Your child may appear clingier than normal.

Acting it out The way children play can give us a lot of information about how they are feeling and can often reflect their mood. You may find that, following a traumatic event, your child will re-enact some of it through play. For example, if your child has witnessed domestic violence over a period of time, this might be expressed through her dolls' role-play, where the dolls are constantly shouting at or hitting one another.

Table 11 PTSD checklist

		Yes	No
1	Are you aware of any significant event or trauma that your child has experienced?		
2	Have you noticed a change in your child's mood? Does he/she seem to be in a low mood or more anxious than usual?		
3	Does your child always seem on edge or jumpy?		
4	Does your child seem visibly anxious at times? Short of breath? Racing heart? Feeling sick? Sweating?		
5	Does your child seem to avoid going to certain places? Does the thought of going somewhere make your child feel intensely anxious?		
6	Does your child describe experiencing flashbacks of the event or trauma?		
7	Have you noticed a change in your child's appetite?		
8	Is there a change in your child's sleep pattern?		
9	Does your child describe hearing voices or sounds that other people can't hear?		

Isolating themselves   Your child may switch off from every-thing going on around him, from you or the rest of the family, from friends or from school. It might be that your child used to be quite loving and affectionate, but has struggled to express affection more recently. Your child may appear more withdrawn than before the incident.

Other ways to cope   Often the symptoms of PTSD can be so difficult for your child to manage that he may try to find other ways of coping. It is not uncommon for children to be tempted by things such as alcohol or cigarettes; they may even turn to illicit drugs to help manage their anxiety. We often forget that food can be used as a drug, as it can be comforting. Equally, this might be the one thing that your child feels he is in control of, so he may resort to restricting what he eats.

Dr Vohra's take-home messages: PTSD

- PTSD is often associated with symptoms of depression and anx-iety. Look back at Chapters 2 and 3 to remind yourself what signs to look out for if you are concerned that your child is presenting as low in mood or anxious.
- Remember that your child's symptoms may not develop im-mediately after a traumatic event has occured; it can take some months or even years before the effects will begin to show them-selves.

Traffic light: green
FACE-FEAR

- Have a face-to-face conversation with your child.
- Be attentive; listen to what your child has to say.
- Stay calm.
- Have you run through the PTSD checklist to get the facts?
- Explain to your child why you are worried.
- Agree an action and, if appropriate, go to amber.

Traffic light: amber

If you are concerned that your child has any of the symptoms described in this chapter, then book an appointment with your GP for the child to be assessed. Avoid asking your child direct questions about possible trauma; this may do more harm than good and can require specialist talking therapy to unpick.

Traffic light: red

Sometimes your child's symptoms may mean that she has thoughts of hurting herself or other people. Your child may have actually acted on these thoughts and self-harmed; if she is known to self-harm, you may have noticed that there is an increase in her self-harming behaviour. If you are concerned that your child is at risk of hurting herself or others, then ensure you seek support promptly. Contact emergency services or take your child to A&E for an urgent assessment.

12

'I'm worried my child is taking drugs'

Jack, 13

Jack's mum has been worried that he always seems so tired and is never motivated to do anything. She finds it a real struggle to even get him out of bed in the morning, let alone get him ready for school. He has had a few late nights recently. He acts shifty when he gets in and never wants to look her straight in the eye. There is always a distinct smell around him, one that she is pretty sure is cannabis. She knows she should say something, but worries that she's got it all wrong and then will plant the idea of taking drugs in his head. She did ask him once if he had been smoking anything he shouldn't have. He denied it, of course, and told her that he had gone to a friend's house and they had all been passing a spliff around. He told her that he'd not even held a spliff, let alone smoked one, but that because he is in the same room as the rest of them, he still comes back smelling of it. She wants to believe him, but he always looks as zonked as the rest of them.

He's put on some weight. He comes back home, with a friend usually, and they camp out in the kitchen and eat their way through family bags of crisps. She is pretty sure it is the post-weed munchies. She is not sure where he is getting his money from to even buy the drugs in the first place; he certainly isn't getting it from her.

The idea of your child taking or misusing either legal or illegal substances can be a source of anxiety, upset, anger and disappointment for parents. Your child may be quite secretive about his or her drug use and this may go unnoticed by you as their parent or carer for some time. It might be that your child doesn't see what she is doing as problematic or it might take an intervention by concerned family and friends before she even sees her behaviour as harmful.

When we think about the term 'drugs', we often think first about illegal substances such as cannabis, cocaine, LSD, ecstasy, magic mushrooms, heroin and so forth. For us professionals, however, substance misuse covers everything – not only illegal substances but also legal ones, including alcohol, tobacco, over-the-counter (OTC) medications and legally prescribed drugs. The latter can be a medication your child is being prescribed or something that you, your partner or a close relative or friend is prescribed.

Drug taking can be an education for doctors as well as parents. As newer and newer drugs reach the market, it is impossible to keep track of the drug lingo and slang or the various street names for individual drugs. Seeing children who use illicit substances can often be a bit of an education for me too. The language around drugs is constantly changing. If there is slang that I don't understand, I normally ask the child to clarify it for me.

Likewise, don't be afraid to ask your child questions and get him to clarify things if you are not sure. Sometimes, as a parent or carer, you may not want your child to see you as out of touch or not streetwise. It is important, however, to get a good understanding of your child and his drug use.

Different types of drugs

- Alcohol.
- Tobacco.
- Aerosols.
- Over-the-counter medications.
- Medication prescribed to the child.
- Medication prescribed to a family member, relative or friend.
- Illegal substances (cannabis, cocaine, LSD, magic mushrooms, heroin).

Is my child using drugs?

Here are some general points to consider when you are thinking about your child's possible drug use.

Accessibility

You might want to think about how easy it is for your child to obtain a particular substance. If alcohol is always available at home and is not locked away, it can be relatively straightforward for your child to get hold of, while illegal, 'harder' substances, such as cocaine, may not be so readily sourced. What about tablets like paracetamol and ibuprofen or prescribed medication? Are these within reach of the whole family? Maybe they are in an unlocked bathroom cabinet or on bedside tables, tucked in handbags or left on kitchen work surfaces?

Money

How is your child funding his habit? Do you give your child a weekly allowance but find there doesn't seem to be anything to show for it? Maybe the child has a part-time job but the pay doesn't seem to stretch very far? It might be that she can't afford to buy the drugs herself, so instead she commits petty crimes to fund her habit.

Bad company?

You can expect your child to fall in and out of friendship groups regularly as she grows older. Have you noticed that she has completely abandoned old friendships? Perhaps you feel uncomfortable about the new company your child is keeping, with unsavoury characters turning up on your doorstep. How open and honest is your child being about his friends and what they get up to? Is he being vague about his plans and refusing to give you contact details for any of the friends he will be with?

Remember what we said about gut instinct – if something feels off, nine times out of ten it is. If you are unsure about new friendships, ask your child about them.

Changes in interest and academic performance

You may notice that your child is less motivated to do things she used to enjoy. For instance, perhaps your child used to enjoy playing hockey or football on a Saturday morning, but nowadays each time the weekend comes round you are faced with another excuse as to why she can't go. Your child's teacher may also describe him as being less focused and less motivated in class. He may not be able to keep on top of his homework, or college or university deadlines, and as a result his grades may be slipping.

> ### Concerns at work
>
> If your child is not at school but in employment, he may be making reckless mistakes at work, turning up drunk or under the influence and unable to focus or operate machinery or equipment. This can obviously put the individual, other people he works with, customers or the general public at significant risk

General demeanour and behaviour

Parents often describe their children as being secretive, spending long periods of time 'out with friends' and giving vague details of their whereabouts. The child may come back smelling of smoke, or there may be very obvious changes in his mood and behaviour. He may appear tired, sluggish and lacking in energy, particularly if you catch him on a comedown. Equally, you might find him to be alert, with boundless energy (more than you would expect at that time of day or in that particular situation).

Your child may appear distracted, or may respond to things that aren't there. Depending on what substance is being abused, she may describe being able to hear or see things that aren't there. She may appear anxious or on edge.

You might ask yourself some other questions: Does your child appear less motivated and more withdrawn than usual? Is he disinhibited, acting inappropriately, laughing over nothing?

Suspicious objects or paraphernalia

However 'careful' your child may be in concealing his behaviour from you, it is often only a matter of time before you come across something that confirms your fear that he is using. You may come across tobacco tins or lighters. Your child may leave suspicious packaging lying around, with remnants of powder or resins. Depending on the substance concerned, you may find other drug paraphernalia such as burnt foil or teaspoons, syringes, empty popper bottles, tins, cut-up plastic bottles or odd-looking pipes. There may be evidence in the form of empty food and drink wrappers that your child has taken drugs, particularly if she has had the 'munchies' afterwards, as is often the case with cannabis and even alcohol.

Forensic history

Is your child getting into trouble more frequently than usual? Have the police been involved? Often drug taking and contact with the police can go hand in hand; your child is more likely to get himself into unlawful situations while under the influence, or may have turned to crime in order to fund his habit.

Physical appearance

Your child's physical appearance can be an indicator of her potential drug use. In general, how does your child look? Has she neglected her self-care and hygiene? Does she appear dishevelled and unkempt? Have you noticed any weight loss or weight gain?

Have you noticed any unusual smells emanating from your child? Does he smell strongly of tobacco, alcohol or cannabis, for instance? Is he making over-the-top attempts to hide odours with air fresheners, overpowering perfumes, mints, chewing gum?

Body scan

Go through our quick body scan checklist. This will give you some idea of what the common signs of drug use are. As always, make sure you look at these in the context of other symptoms and what else is going on in the child's life. Just because her eyes are red, for instance, doesn't automatically mean she is using illegal substances.

Table 12 Body scan checklist

	Yes	No
Head		
1 Does your child appear drowsy, confused or 'out of it'?		
2 Is your child more forgetful than normal?		
3 Is your child struggling to focus and concentrate?		
4 Thinking about your child's head, has he/she experienced any fits recently when he/she is normally fit and well?		
5 Look at your child's eyes. Are they bloodshot? How about the pupils (the black in your child's eyes)? Are they unusually small or large?		
6 Have you noticed your child is using eye drops to reduce puffiness and redness?		
7 Is your child's speech slurred?		
8 Is your child clenching his/her jaw more than normal?		
9 Is your child experiencing frequent nosebleeds?		
Arms/torso		
1 Are there any unusual markings on your child's arm? Needle puncture wounds (track marks)?		
2 Has your child had any unusual injuries?		
3 Does your child have any unexplained bruises?		
Legs		
1 Is your child unsteady on his/her feet?		
2 Again, think about any unexplained or unusual injuries and bruising.		

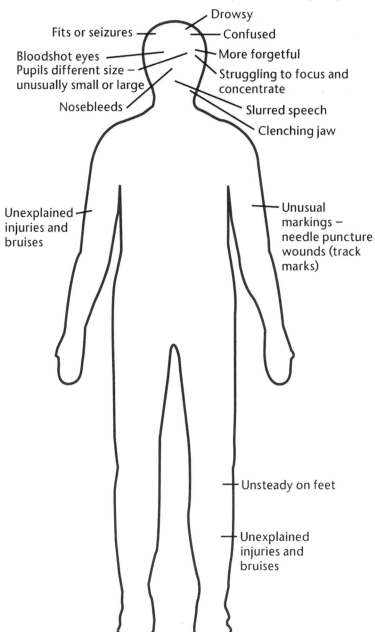

Figure 2 Substance misuse checklist

Table 13 Substance misuse checklist

	Yes	No
1 Has your child begun acting secretively?		
2 Has your child got a new circle of friends?		
3 Is your gut telling you to be worried?		
4 Is your child asking you for more money with seemingly nothing to show for it?		
5 Have you noticed that money or valuables have gone missing around the house?		
6 Is your child falling behind at school, college or university?		
7 Has anyone else flagged up concerns about your child?		
8 Have you noticed any unusual smells coming from your child or his/her room?		
9 Have you spotted any unusual objects or drug paraphernalia?		
10 Have you noticed any changes in your child's mood or behaviour?		
11 Does your child appear to be hearing or seeing things that aren't there?		
12 Is your child making less effort with his/her physical appearance than usual?		
13 Does your child seem to be physically unwell more often than in the past?		
14 Does your child seem to be taking more risks and getting into trouble with the police more than before?		

Dr Vohra's take-home messages: substance misuse

- Trust your gut and your sense of smell. If you think something is amiss, it normally is.
- Often it can be really frightening to catch your child under the influence of drugs or in a state after drug use. If this happens,

you may not know the right thing to say or do. As always, it is important to be upfront and honest with your child. Be explicit. If you smell tobacco, let the child know that is what you smell. It gives your worries some context.

Traffic light: green
FACE-FEAR

- Have a face-to-face conversation with your child.
- Be attentive; listen to what your child has to say.
- Stay calm.
- Have you run through the substance misuse checklist to get the facts?
- Explain to your child why you are worried.
- Agree an action and, if appropriate, go to amber.

Traffic light: amber
If you are worried that your child has become dependent on drugs or alcohol, it is likely the child will not see his or her drug use as a problem. Encourage your child to book an appointment with your GP if he or she is old enough or at the very least join you for an appointment.

Traffic light: red
If you have immediate concerns about your child's physical health, then take him or her to A&E or contact emergency services. As described, depending on the substance he has taken, the child may behave in a way that puts himself or others at risk of harm. Perhaps the child is heavily under the influence and throwing himself in front of traffic? He may experience crashes in mood during which he has thoughts of hurting himself or other people. He may have actually acted on these thoughts and self-harmed; if the child is known to self-harm, you may have noticed that there is an increase in his self-harming behaviour. If you are concerned that your child is at risk of hurting himself or others, then ensure you seek support promptly. Contact emergency services or take your child to A&E for an urgent assessment.

13

'I'm worried my child is grieving'

Tom, 12
Tom has had no previous involvement with mental health services. Other than for his usual developmental checks, his parents have never needed to take him to the GP. His parents are in the throes of a divorce. Tom has known for some time that something was going on between them. The giveaway was Dad sleeping downstairs on the sofa, but he would always brush it off as accidentally falling asleep in front of the TV. Tom's worst fears were confirmed when he caught Mum and Dad having a full-on argument when he came back from school one day. Nan tried to shoo him out the way, but he had already seen the worst of it. Not long after that, his parents sat him down to explain that they had not been happy for a while and were really struggling to keep it together, but had wanted to for his sake.

Tom seemed to take the news quite well at first, as well as a boy his age could. If he was honest, he couldn't quite believe it was happening. He remembers laughing at them in disbelief when they first told him.

After that, Tom spent time between the family home and Dad's one-bed flat. It was exciting at first – two beds, two lots of toys and no fighting. A couple of months passed and Tom started to feel angry about the whole situation – 'Why me?' All of his friends got to spend the weekend with their whole family, yet his parents couldn't stand to be in the same room, let alone live together. Then came the change in his behaviour. His mum noticed that he seemed angry all the time: he was picking fights left, right and centre, throwing tantrums and wobblers that would give his toddler self a run for his money.

What is grief?

At some point in our lives, we will all experience loss. It might be the end of a relationship, the divorce of your parents or the death of a loved one; these are just some examples. Grief can affect anyone at any age. It is really important to recognize that grief affects everyone differently. What can often be an additional challenge for parents is balancing their own grief reaction with being emotionally available to deal with what their child is going through, particularly when an event has occurred that affects the whole family.

Parental divorce can be very difficult. As parents, you may have had some time to come to terms with the fact that your relationship has ended and have already come through the grieving process yourselves, either wholly or to some extent, by the time your child finds out about the situation. Your child will, more than likely, be emotional and confused. She may want to cry, scream or shout. As a parent, it is understandable that you will experience a lot of guilt about your decision, feeling on some level that you have caused your child's pain.

It is important to give your child the space she needs to process the information properly. Give your child time to speak. If she wants to scream and shout about it, let her. Obviously if your child is doing something that puts herself or others at risk of harm, then it is important to seek professional support early on.

Causes of a grief reaction

Grief is often associated with death but, as I mentioned above, a number of things can cause your child to experience a grief reaction. These include:

- the death of a loved one;
- the death of a friend;
- the death of a pet;
- the end of a relationship;
- parental divorce;
- the end of a school year.

It is normal for us to 'grieve' for any one of the above. Grief is, by its very nature, a normal response to loss. It stops being a normal reaction, however, if it goes on for a long time and there are other mental health symptoms associated with it.

Normal grief reaction

We all go through different stages of grief and this is no different for your child. We will go through each of these stages at our own pace and may, in fact, move forwards and backwards through the stages rather than follow a sequential pattern. It is really helpful, as parents, to recognize what a normal grief reaction looks like, so that when your child experiences each of the stages described, you are not taken aback. Most people prepare themselves for sadness and tears, but they don't quite expect the shock and anger that can also be a part of the grieving process. At times, it can feel like an emotional rollercoaster.

Denial

Your child's initial response to the loss might be disbelief that it is even happening. She can't get her head round it and she is in denial. It doesn't seem real to her. It is important that you support and re-assure your child through this stage. It might be that in her disbelief she will try to search for a loved one who has passed away or may think the person concerned will be coming back at some point. This can be very distressing for you as a parent, especially if you are trying to come to terms with the loss yourself, but it is important not to 'play along' with your child's belief that the deceased person or pet, for instance, is coming back. Be sure to keep sensitively explaining what has happened to the deceased person in simple terms and in a language that you know your child will understand. If the child is young, you might explain that a loved one 'has gone to heaven and has been given his angel wings'. If your child is a teenager, you will probably change the wording you use to be more in keeping with how you would speak with an adult.

Anger

After the disbelief and denial stage, your child will often move through to the anger phase. She may ask questions such as, 'Why me?' - in other words, 'Why was it me who had to lose a parent or whose parents had to separate?' She may express her anger physically or with the words she uses. She may hit out at you, others around her or inanimate objects in her environment. She may even show her anger through her play. She may be more destructive while playing with her toys or when role playing with her dolls or action heroes. You may notice she throws more tantrums.

Managing anger as a result of grief

As mentioned above, it is important to allow your child to express how he or she feels. If, however, her anger could result in harm coming to her or those around her, it is equally important to intervene. Reassure your child that it is OK to feel angry at what has happened, but it is not OK to hit people.

If your child is in his teens, his anger may take the form of rebellion. He may start truanting from school, get into scraps with his peers or play up in class. He may direct his anger towards hospital staff who he feels didn't do enough to save his loved one. It might be that he doesn't know how to manage these emotions and looks at ways to numb the pain they cause, perhaps through alcohol or experimenting with drugs.

Bargaining

To describe what 'bargaining means', I will use the example of parental divorce. Your child might be so desperate for his parents to get back together that he would be willing to do anything. Sometimes children – and particularly younger children – may question if it's something they have done that has led to their parents separating: 'Are Mummy and Daddy separating because I've been naughty? I promise I'll be good from now on and do what I am told.' They may promise they will tidy their room from now on, for example, without having to be nagged about it, if it means that it will bring the family back together.

Similarly, if your child is grieving for the loss of a friend, parent or loved one, she may experience feelings of guilt and the 'if only's': 'If only I had behaved better, then this wouldn't have happened.'

This phase tends to be short-lived and you can expect your child to come through it as she comes to terms with her loss.

Depression

As a parent, you would expect your child to feel upset or down when he has experienced a loss. This often suggests that he has come to terms with the loss, that he understands the person or pet is gone for good and isn't coming back. He might acknowledge that Mummy and Daddy are not getting back together. He may finally realize that any attempt he makes at trying to bargain, the 'if only's', won't work. This may leave your child feeling helpless, which, in turn, will make him feel low.

Guilt

Your child may feel guilty that a relationship has come to an end or a loved one has passed away. This, again, is a normal response to loss. It is important that you reassure your child this is in no way her fault. If she is old enough, explain to her what has happened and why it has happened.

Language

Make sure the language that you use is appropriate for your child's age and only give your child as much information as is absolutely necessary. Make some attempt first to find out from your child why he feels guilty. Let him speak to you in his own language. This will give some direction to your conversation, as you can address each of your child's concerns in turn.

Acceptance

As your child continues to grieve, she will ultimately reach a stage where she comes to terms with what has happened. She will realize that Mummy and Daddy are not going to get back together, Goldie has gone for good or Great-grandma is never coming back. She may verbalize this by explaining where Goldie has gone in her language - 'Goldie has gone to heaven'. It might be that you see less of the bargaining and her mood is brighter.

A summary of the grieving process

- Denial
- Anger
- Bargaining
- Depression
- Acceptance

Disruptions to routine

As we know from earlier chapters, our mood – that is, the way we feel – often affects other aspects of our life: our concentration, relationships, working life, sleep, appetite and so on. You may notice that your child's sleep has been more disturbed than normal since he learned of the loss. He may find it difficult to get off to sleep and need you to sit with him or soothe him; he may require a bedside lamp or nightlight to be left on. He may need reassurance that you are not going anywhere. It might be that getting to sleep isn't the problem; the real struggle may be staying asleep. Your child may be restless and/or get up several times in the night.

Lack of appetite

As we know all too well, food can often be used as an emotional crutch at times of anguish and grief. Your child may turn to food for comfort or the reverse might happen and he might lose his appetite and it is a real struggle to get him to eat anything. You may have concerns about your child's weight. It can be difficult when the family is grieving to stick to any sort of routine. It is important in among the grief that you ensure that, whenever possible, there is some normality around things like mealtimes and sleep.

Dr Vohra's take-home messages: grief

- Be prepared for your child to experience a real rollercoaster of emotions in response to grief.
- While you should support your child in expressing his or her feelings, seek professional support if you have concerns that the child is becoming a risk to himself or others in the process.

Traffic light: green

FACE-FEAR

- Have a face-to-face conversation with your child.
- Be attentive; listen to what your child has to say.
- Stay calm.
- Explain to your child why you are worried.
- Agree an action and, if appropriate, go to amber.

Traffic light: amber

While we never fully get over a loss, there is an expectation that the symptoms of grief should settle with time. If you are worried that your child's symptoms are getting worse or no better, it is important to book her in to see your GP. Her symptoms may be interfering with her everyday life, affecting relationships with family or friends or her school attendance. In complicated grief reactions, your child may also be constantly preoccupied with thinking about the loss. She may even see or hear the deceased. This can obviously be a frightening and upsetting experience.

Traffic light: red

Sometimes your child's symptoms may mean that she has thoughts of hurting herself or other people. Your child may have actually acted on these thoughts and self-harmed; if the child is known to self-harm, you may have noticed that there is an increase in her self-harming behaviour. If you are concerned that your child is at risk of hurting herself or others, then ensure you seek support promptly. Contact emergency services or take your child to A&E for an urgent assessment.

14

'I'm worried about my child's sleep'

Parents and carers commonly seek advice from their GP about their child's sleep. They may be worried that their child isn't getting enough, or is sleeping too much. They may be concerned that their child can't get off to sleep, or that when the child does go to sleep, she wakes up frequently in the night.

What's your child's routine?

Children I see will often say they are struggling to get to sleep, but when they describe their bedtime routine it is no wonder – they are often watching box sets until the early hours of the morning or flitting from one social media account to another. At the first appointment, I will always try to get a sense of what a normal night-time routine looks like at home. A poor night-time routine can have a huge impact on your child's ability not only to get to sleep but also stay asleep for a decent length of time, and for this sleep to be restful. You can get an idea of what your child's night-time routine is like by filling in the checklist in Table 14. It will help you identify some simple measures you can put in place at home that may help your child get a better night's sleep.

If you have answered 'Yes' to one or more of the questions in the checklist in Table 14, then there are likely to be small changes you can make to your child's routine that will make a difference.

What can you do to help your child sleep better?

Make sure your child goes to bed at the same time each night
In the week during term-time, your child may already have a good routine. She goes to bed at a reasonable time and is up early the

Table 14 Night routine checklist

	Yes	No
1 Does your child struggle to get off to or stay asleep? Does your child regularly wake up early? Does he/she experience a combination of all these?		
2 Does your child go to bed at the same time each night?		
3 Does your child drink lots of caffeinated drinks throughout the day and into the evening?		
4 Does your child watch TV, play on his/her phone, play video games or watch services like Netflix before bed?		

following morning in time for school. Come the weekend or during the holidays, however, perhaps your child is suddenly given free rein to do what she wants. She decides to go to sleep the other side of midnight and lies in until midday the following day. Before she knows it, Monday morning or the start of the school term comes round and her body clock is out of sync.

It is amazing how much of an impact a couple of days out of routine can have on your child's overall physical and mental wellbeing. It is important for her to have some semblance of a routine, regardless of whether it is a weekday or a weekend, term-time or the holidays. Poor routines at the weekend can undo the good work you put into the week, so make sure your child's routine is consistent. Make sure she goes to sleep at the same time each night and wakes up at the same time each day, whether it is during the week or at the weekend.

Make sure that caffeinated drinks are kept to a minimum
High-sugar, caffeinated energy drinks seem to be all the rage at the minute. You only have to watch kids downing them on their way to school to realize how much they are relied on as a quick energy boost. Your child may drink several of these in a day without any particular cut-off time. The danger comes when the child drinks them later on in the day. Caffeine stimulates the mind, keeping it

active - the complete opposite of what is needed to unwind and get ready for bed. This means that your child's brain never gets the cue to tell him that it is time to sleep.

Try to encourage your child to steer clear of these drinks in the evening. Set a cut-off time of 4 p.m. If he must have a hot drink later on in the day, try a decaffeinated equivalent instead. Things like cola, tea, coffee and chocolate are other common culprits. Limit your child's consumption of these later on in the day or, again, switch to decaffeinated options.

Limit your child's screen time As well as having a caffeine curfew, it is important to have a cut-off for your child's screen time too. As a parent myself, I understand only too well that this is easier said than done. It can be hard enough as adults to put our phones down - there is always someone to text, ring or send an instant message to - but is even harder for children and young adults to do so. Think about how stimulating all these activities can be, though, not only because they involve actively reading messages and replying to them but also by how illuminated, coloured screens and moving pictures continue to stimulate our brains when, really, they ought to be switching off.

Think about cutting out all screens an hour before bed as a starting point. This includes phones, TVs and computers. Get your child into the habit of going up to his bedroom an hour before lights out. Remove all temptation wherever possible by avoiding putting a TV or computer in your child's room and charging any phones elsewhere. Encourage your child to read a book or a magazine for a little while before bed instead. If he isn't keen on that, suggest that he listen to some music that is mellow rather than of the heavy metal variety!

I'm not going to pretend that this will be easy for you or your child, particularly if he is a bit of a screen junkie. Wherever possible, however, I avoid prescribing medication to help with your children's sleep and the recommendations given above are ones that your GP or your child's psychiatrist would also suggest you put in place before medication would be mentioned.

Even if medication is considered, it is unlikely to work effectively if your child isn't practising the good sleep habits suggested above to complement it. Often children and their parents are surprised that sleeping still appears to be a struggle even with the addition of medication. When we unpick this further, it usually becomes clear that the medication is fighting a losing battle with late nights, caffeine and electronic gadgets.

Is the child's room dark enough? When the lighter summer nights come around, it can often be difficult to convince your child that it is late enough for him to go to sleep. Blackout blinds have been a saviour in our house! On the simplest of levels, children associate darkness with sleep and light with day. For younger children in particular, blackout blinds are a good investment. For older children, perhaps you could try eye masks.

Avoid exercise before bed Regular exercise is important for both your child's physical health and overall mental well-being, but she should try to avoid working out immediately before bed. Usually, exercising right before bed is quite stimulating and will keep the mind active, which is not what you want when you're trying to go to sleep.

Don't nap in the day The knock-on effect of poor sleep is that your child or teen may choose to nap in the day to 'catch up'. This is generally best avoided as it knocks your child's natural sleep rhythm out of sync.

Dr Vohra's take-home messages: sleeping problems

- Encourage your child to go to bed at the same time each night and get up at the same time each morning, whether it is a weekday or a weekend.
- Make sure that the child's room is dark enough.
- Your child should avoid napping during the day.
- Your child should avoid caffeinated drinks too late in the day.
- Cut back on your child's screen time in the evening.

15

'I'm worried my child may be being abused'

We hear so much in the media about child abuse. It is one of the most incomprehensible things that can happen to a child. Indeed, for your child to be the victim of abuse can be one of the most distressing and damaging things that can happen to the family as a whole.

There are many forms of abuse, but the ones you will most commonly have heard of include:

- physical abuse
- sexual abuse
- emotional abuse
- neglect.

There is a huge amount of sensitivity surrounding the issue of abuse and what can make it all the more difficult is that your child may be unaware what is happening to him is wrong. He may find it difficult to come forward about it, particularly if the abuser is known to the family. This reluctance may be due to threats from the abuser or the fear of not being believed.

Obviously, depending on the type of abuse, some signs may be more obvious than others. As ever, always trust your gut instinct. It can be all too easy to assume that you are worrying about nothing, overreacting, reading too much into things, but if you suspect something is amiss it normally is.

Physical abuse

If your child has an injury for which there is no obvious explanation or if the story behind the injury doesn't quite fit, then this can often ring alarm bells and may be an indicator of physical abuse.

Bumps and bruises

Growing up you expect children to get the occasional knock, bump or bruise, but usually you can link their injuries to some sort of explanation:

> 'I've got a bruise on my leg because someone whacked me with a hockey stick.'
> 'I sprained my ankle playing football.'

If your child is learning to walk, a bump here and a bump there is not uncommon.

Other signs of physical injury that may indicate abuse

Bruises are not the only signs of physical injury. It may be that your child is in and out of hospital with broken bones or repeated burns. You may notice burns in several areas. It might be a scald from a hot drink or a burn from the end of a cigarette; unusual markings should arouse suspicion.

Parents of a five-month-old boy have brought him to A&E where he has a burn all down his right arm. His parents have told staff that he stood up and pulled a hot cup of tea over himself. The members of staff are suspicious as, while the little boy has been in the department, it is obvious that he can barely sit up, let alone pull himself to standing.

Healthcare professionals will often have a degree of suspicion if an injury doesn't seem to fit with the story given. In the case above, it was obvious to the members of staff that the young boy was developmentally too young to stand, so how could he pull a cup of tea over himself?

Emotional abuse

Emotional abuse can often be the subtlest form of abuse and the hardest to pick up on. Your child may be constantly being put down, criticized or ignored. Perhaps your child is never praised or the perpetrator of abuse (the abuser) never shows the child any affection. It might be that your child is repeatedly called names or degraded. She may be constantly rejected or deliberately excluded. For instance, if the perpetrator of the abuse has contact with other children, he may treat them to trips out or reward them for good behaviour, while showing the victim of abuse the opposite treatment.

Sexual abuse

Sexual abuse can include anything from your child being groomed on the internet by the perpetrator or abuser to engaging in sexual activities. Another area that is fast being recognized as a mode of sexual abuse is the sharing of explicit images. There has been a sharp increase in more recent years in the numbers of children sharing images with their abusers through social media. The child might be forced into sending explicit photos of herself via instant messaging. It may be that she is coerced into engaging in sexual activities via webcam. Children may become trapped in a vicious cycle of abuse from which there is seemingly no escape, particularly if the perpetrator uses threats as a means of control: 'If you don't do what I tell you, then I will do X, Y or Z.' The perpetrator may threaten to show other people images that the child has sent of herself or convince her that no one will believe her story.

The perpetrator of the sexual abuse may start to befriend the child early on and 'groom' the child over a period of time. This allows the perpetrator to build a connection and gain the child's trust, which makes it more likely that the child will say or do what the perpetrator has asked of him.

The signs of sexual abuse may not be immediately obvious to even the most perceptive of parents. The signs can manifest as anything from physical marks right through to emotional scars. Depending on the age of your child, some signs may be easier to pick up on than others. For instance, physical marks from sexual abuse may be more noticeable in a child who you are still washing, dressing and undressing, whereas if your child is a lot more independent, it may be difficult to pick up on such signs. A troubling sign that a child is possibly being sexually abused is that he wets or soils himself, particularly if he has previously been dry and accident free. The most obvious sign of sexual abuse may be pregnancy in a girl who you do not believe to be sexually active.

Your child may report that she is sore down below. There may be signs of force, such as vaginal or anal tears. It may be that the child has picked up a sexually transmitted infection (STI), which, again, for children of a certain age would undoubtedly ring alarm bells. Your child may have noticed some unusual discharge coming from down below.

Emotional indicators of sexual abuse

Your child may appear frightened when in the vicinity of his abuser. He may avoid places, specific days or times when he knows the abuser will be around. As a parent, you may notice a pattern to this. You may even confront your child, only to find he appears too frightened to say anything about it.

Oversexualized behaviour – a sign of abuse?

Often we think about children being more withdrawn than normal as the result of abuse. It is not uncommon for children who have been sexually abused to present as overly sexualized instead, however. Your child may have an understanding of sex that is way beyond what would be expected for her years. This can be quite alarming.

Neglect

As parents, we have a responsibility to make sure that our children's basic needs (food, warmth and security) are being met. If a child is being consistently and repeatedly denied those things, then we start to think that child is being neglected. The common signs, and the most obvious to spot, are likely to manifest in how the child appears to you.

- Does the child appear clean? Is she grubby? Is she always like this?
- Are the child's clothes clean? Do they appear to have been washed at all?

- Is the child wearing the right clothes for the season? Does he seem underdressed in the cold? Is he lacking the essentials that all children ought to have?
- Does the child appear malnourished? Is she getting enough to eat or does she appear hungry and underweight?
- Is the child being taken to the doctor if he is unwell? Is he missing appointments?
- Is the child shown love and affection or does she constantly seem to be vying for it? Is she being left repeatedly unsupervised at home alone?
- Does the child always seem to be having accidents?
- Is the child living in squalor? Are her surroundings dangerous? Might she come to serious harm?
- Does the child always seem to be unwell?

If neglect, whether physical or emotional, continues for a prolonged period of time, particularly in younger children, it can

Signs of abuse

It is not always easy to work out what type of abuse a child is being subjected to. It is often the case that there is a change in the child's behaviour, which, in turn, leads to a parent or carer expressing concern. Here are some general signs a concerned parent or carer might notice.

- The child seems a lot quieter than normal, when usually you can't get her to sit still and stop talking.
- You may notice he seems more down than normal when usually he is relatively happy.
- A child who has always been a good sleeper has recently begun waking up in a cold sweat, having nightmares and struggling to get off to and stay asleep.
- The child may seem clingier than normal and need to be constantly reassured. The child may not settle off to sleep without you near him.
- You may notice that she is off her food. She may have lost a lot of weight in a short space of time or, on the contrary, gained weight through comfort eating.

start to affect the child's development. A child who is deprived of food, for instance, may be very underweight and shorter than others her age. If a child is subjected to emotional neglect, he may fall behind with his social skills or have delays in the development of his speech. Neglect may even affect the way the child moves, so, for example, a child you would expect to be walking confidently by a certain age may show no signs that she is even ready to start walking.

Spotting signs of abuse

Some of the problems we looked at in earlier chapters may also indicate that a child is being abused. They include the following.

Self-harm

Sometimes children find it difficult to cope with feelings of distress and anxiety. They may look at other ways to manage these emotions. They may start self-harming or, if they are known to self-harm already, they may be doing it more often. As discussed in earlier chapters, self-harm covers a whole host of different behaviours from taking an overdose to self-cutting, self-punching or biting.

Drugs and alcohol

Some children may turn to drugs and alcohol to help them cope. Growing up, you might expect children and young people to experiment with drugs and alcohol, but when this is repeated over and over again and to excess – to the point that it is causing the child harm or putting her in risky situations – then it is important to consider the reasons behind this.

Level of functioning

How is your child coping with day-to-day life? Has there been a change in her behaviour towards other family members? She may seem more distant than normal. She may find it difficult to cope with the demands of daily life. She may cut off friends. She may struggle to get into school and have days, weeks or even months off at a time when usually her attendance is 100 per cent.

Dr Vohra's take-home messages: abuse

- It is important that you do not look at the signs described above in isolation. Consider them within the context of what else is going on.
- Trust your gut instinct; it is there for a reason. If something feels off or you have significant concerns about your child, make sure you act on these - don't ignore or dismiss them.
- Talk to your child. Give the child time to explain things from his own perspective. Be patient and don't expect to hear it all, if anything, from one conversation alone. Your child needs to feel safe before she is able to share what is happening to her.

Traffic light: green

FACE-FEAR

- Have a face-to-face conversation with your child.
- Be attentive; listen to what your child has to say.
- Stay calm.
- Explain to your child why you are worried.
- Agree an action and, if appropriate, go to amber.

Traffic light: amber

If you are concerned that your own child, or another child you know, may be a victim of abuse, contact your local council's social care/social services duty team for advice. You may not know for certain that a child is being abused, but it is always helpful to run your concerns past the team to see if they are able to assist in supporting your child and the family. The team may consider whether or not your child needs to be allocated a social worker to assess the concerns further. In some cases, they may refer the case on to the police for investigation.

Traffic light: red

If you are concerned that your child is in immediate danger as a result of abuse, then contact the police.

Sometimes your child's symptoms may mean that he has thoughts of hurting himself or other people. The child may have actually acted on these thoughts and self-harmed; if he is known to self-harm already, you may have noticed that there is an increase in his self-harming behaviour. If you are concerned that your child is at risk of hurting himself or others, then ensure you seek support promptly. Contact emergency services or take your child to A&E for an urgent assessment.

16

'I'm worried my child is being bullied'

As a parent myself, I understand only too well that feeling of worry, wondering how your child will get on at school and, more specifically, with other kids. If you are very anxious, this may come from your own experiences of school. Perhaps you were bullied or knew someone who was. Maybe you were a bully yourself and feel remorse for your behaviour, yet still worry that your own child may be on the receiving end.

How has bullying evolved? It may not be immediately obvious that your child is being bullied. In this age of social media, bullying is not only carried out face to face in the playground but can also extend out of school time to include prank phone calls, abusive text messages and demeaning exchanges over social media platforms.

Much like abuse, bullying can take a number of forms, which can be psychological or physical.

Emotional bullying

Emotional or psychological bullying can take the form of repeated name calling or constant put-downs. The bully may use intimidation to get a rise out of her victim. She may poke fun at your child's mannerisms or mimic the child's behaviour and look to others around her to laugh or join in. Sometimes something as simple as the body language a bully uses can be enough to frighten your child. He may constantly look at your child in a menacing way or with contempt. It might be that the bully goes to extreme ends to humiliate your child by spreading rumours about her or purposefully excluding her from activities. The bully may try to get a rise out of your child by talking about his friends and family in a derogatory way.

Physical bullying

Physical bullying is probably the most obvious form of bullying, particularly if your child is coming home battered and bruised. She may be limping, clutching her side or have taken some knocks to the face that suggest she has been in a fight. It might be that the bully throws his weight about by punching or kicking your child; he may trip your child over.

Bullying is wrong

The worst advice you can give a child who is being bullied are choice phrases such as, 'If it doesn't break you, it will make you stronger', 'Toughen up' or 'Ignore them and they will get bored.' This can undermine your child's feelings and may put up barriers to future conversations. Ultimately, no one should have to put up with bullying. It is not a 'normal part of school experience'. There are no two ways about it: bullying in any shape or form is wrong and your child should not feel that he has to put up with it or stick it out.

What to do if your child is being bullied

It can be very tempting, as a parent, to be riled up with emotion if your child confides in you that she is being bullied. More often than not, though, your child is wanting to offload her experiences to you without having you frogmarch her to school and stand her in front of the head to 'grass up' the bully. Make sure you don't act in haste – and listen to your child.

Getting the facts

It will be helpful to ask your child the following questions.

- How long has this been going on for?
- Who is the bully? Is it one person or several?
- When did it start?
- Why did it start?
- Did you do anything that may have triggered the bullying or spurred the bully on?

This is not about apportioning blame but establishing the facts and a clear sequence of events.

Your child may be able to pinpoint why the bullying started in the first place. Perhaps he and the bully were friends and the friendship turned sour. Often children are unable to explain any possible triggers and, in most cases, bullying can be quite sporadic or seemingly transpire from nothing.

Ask your child what has been happening

A useful tip is to keep a diary of the bullying incidents – when did they happen, who was there and what injuries (including emotional ones) were inflicted? Similarly, with text messages, it is a good idea to keep a log of these, what was said by the bully and what response, if any, your child gave. If the bully is publicly shaming your child on social media, take a screenshot of the pages concerned. This is always useful to have to hand in case the bully takes the material down from the internet.

Rather than rush off with your own assumed agenda, ask your child what she would like you to do with the information she has shared with you. Does she want you to just keep an eye on things or help her by confronting the school, the bully or perhaps the bully's parent or carer, if known?

Dr Vohra's take-home messages: bullying

- Remember, no one should have to put up with bullying. It is not a 'normal part of school experience'. Bullying in any shape or form is wrong.
- Bullying may not always be immediately obvious to you as a parent. Bullying can often be done discreetly via text message, nuisance calls and attacks through social media.

17

'I'm worried my child is shutting me out'

We can all struggle with change. Throughout childhood your child will go through a number of changes or transitions. School or educational transitions are the most obvious examples, with your child moving from nursery to primary school, from primary to secondary, and from secondary to employment, college or university.

It can be hard for a child to adjust to a new environment, new people and new friendship circles. She is moving from the known to the unknown. When your child has mental health difficulties, these periods of adjustment can feel even more overwhelming and difficult.

Exerting their independence

While you want to encourage your child to be independent, it can be really difficult to get your head round the idea that he 'doesn't need me any more'. Often when children move out of the family home - to go to university, for instance - they may register with a different GP. It can be unnerving for a parent to suddenly be shut out of a significant aspect of their child's life. Up until that point, you may have been used to accompanying your child to GP or healthcare appointments. Suddenly your child may not want to share information with you; he may request that you don't join him for appointments.

University: getting used to being kept at arm's length

It can be quite unnerving, when their offspring go away to university, for parents to go from seeing them every day and every night to only seeing them in the holidays, once every 12 weeks. Telephone

The confidentiality agreement

When your child turns 18, there is no expectation that she needs to bring her parents to an appointment or even that she needs to share the details of the appointment with you. As doctors, we must respect your son or daughter's rights to confidentiality. Be assured that if your child were to share information suggesting he or she was at risk of coming to harm or others might come to harm as a result of his or her actions, then we would have a duty of care to break that confidentiality and share this information with you and anyone else who may be directly affected.

contact is often guided by your child and parents I speak to really struggle with the idea that they can go weeks without holding anything that even resembles a proper conversation with their son or daughter. As we established in the earlier chapters, communication with your child is key, as is the quality of the communication between you when you do speak. Insist that you see your son or daughter. This may not have to be in person, but in this technological age, ask her to Facetime, Skype, WhatsApp or Viber you so that when you do chat to her, you can see her as well.

How does your child look?

Physical appearance is always a very useful indicator of how someone is doing mentally and is routinely used by psychiatrists when assessing someone. We have covered physical appearance in earlier chapters, but let's do a quick recap.

General appearance How does your son or daughter appear? Is she looking after herself? Does he appear clean? Obviously we are all entitled to our 'off days', but think: does this keep happening? Every time you ring your daughter, does she always seem unwashed, unkempt, as if she is not taking care of herself? This may seem even more obvious if your son or daughter normally takes pride in looking good.

Signs of tiredness Does your son or daughter appear tired? You would expect tiredness to be the norm for all students, particularly as they get used to the obligatory nights out within the first few months of starting university, when the novelty of going out has not quite worn off. If tiredness persists month in month out, then it may indicate that something else is going on, particularly in the context of any other symptoms.

Under the influence?   It might be that when you do catch up with your child he always seems to be drunk, high, on edge or paranoid. Any unusual behaviour should arouse some level of suspicion or concern.

Eye contact   Is your daughter able to look you in the eye? Does she appear shifty? Is her face covered up?

Behaviour   Does your son or daughter appear restless or on edge? She may be frantically pacing and apparently unable to settle. Is she always on the go?

Signs of distraction   Does your son or daughter appear distracted? Do you get the sense that you don't have his full attention? Is he looking around at things that are not there? Is she calling out or speaking to herself? Does she appear paranoid to you?

Speech   How is your son or daughter's speech? Can you understand what he is saying? He may be struggling to get his words out or may be talking too quickly, flitting from one topic of conversation to the next. Is she slurring her words? Can you make sense of what she is saying? Is she making up words or using them in the wrong context?

Mood   How does your offspring's mood appear to you? Does he seem more down than usual? Perhaps you have noticed that he has lots of energy and is unusually high or happy? Consider whether this is a change from the norm and if it is a consistent change. Obviously we all feel down now and again, but this is more often than not short-lived and can normally be explained by something.

Appetite   How is your offspring's diet? There is a perception that students survive on junk, particularly as they have free rein to eat what they want, when they want, but have you noticed any dramatic changes in your son or daughter's weight? Perhaps she is becoming incredibly fussy about food or no longer joins the family at mealtimes when she is home.

Sleep   How is your son or daughter sleeping, if at all? When she is back for the holidays, does she sleep at times you would expect? Is he getting enough sleep or does he appear to be surviving on very little? Perhaps things have gone the other way and she is sleeping too much. Again, there is an expectation, certainly as your child hits her adolescent years, that she is more likely to go to bed late and rise later in the day but, as with any of the above symptoms, is this a change from the norm?

What have other people said?   Has anyone else expressed concerns about your child? Your worries as a parent can often feel validated if you have another family relative or friend who shares your concerns. It might be that a grandparent has not seen your child for a while, but when they do, typically at some sort of family gathering, they may share some of their own concerns:

'Isn't X a lot snappier than normal?'
'Hasn't he lost some weight?'

Dr Vohra's take-home messages: feeling shut out

- You know your child better than anyone. As healthcare professionals we are often guided by the family's concerns over their child's behaviour.
- Think about the changes you have noticed and over what time period, then relay these to your doctor.

18

'I'm worried my child has body image issues'

As adults we know only too well how much value is placed on how we look. It can be all too easy for your child's confidence to be knocked by an insensitive comment from a friend, family member or peer. If someone comments on your child's weight or height, it can make a lasting impression on him and he may develop a complex. He may wear certain clothes that avoid attention being drawn to that particular body part.

As a mum to a young girl, I am starting to be conscious of how my own actions may be perceived by her. Ultimately, children model themselves on their parents. If your child sees you constantly referring to yourself as 'fat' or checking yourself over and over again in the mirror, some of that behaviour will inevitably rub off on her. Similarly, using the word 'diet' in front of your impressionable teenage girl is going to introduce her to the idea that food is something which ought to be restricted.

Make sure you use positive words to describe yourself (even if you don't believe them!) It is important to empower your child to embrace his body hang-ups; it is also important to 'model' or show your child that you are body confident – you realize that your body may not be perfect, but you accept and embrace every perceived flaw.

People underestimate the importance of a positive body image. If we feel good about ourselves, it will be reflected in our overall mental well-being. If your child has a body hang-up or feelings of low self-esteem, this will consume him and affect how he goes about his daily life. He may not want to go out because of his perceived body hang-up. She may not socialize as much as she used to, making her feel worse off and feeding further into her low self-esteem. This is a very crude example, but allows you to get a sense of how things can spiral.

All shapes and sizes

It is important to highlight to your child that beauty comes in all shapes and sizes. It sounds very clichéd, but identifying a handful of people in the public eye who vary in height, build and weight (make them relatable to your child - that is, celebrities your child will know) will reinforce the message that you don't have to be a certain size in order to be 'beautiful'. In a world of unpoliced social media, Photoshopped 'ideal' images may be what your child aspires to achieve but these are not realistic.

If you do talk about food or body ideals, again make sure your focus is positive. Rather than viewing food as something that needs to be controlled, limited or portioned, it is important to train your child into focusing on eating for health. If your child makes sensible food choices and focuses on the quality of food he is getting, then the rest will fall into place. Stop referring to foods as either good or bad, as this will instil in your child the need to restrict certain food groups.

If you notice that your son or daughter is constantly putting him- or herself down, constantly placing value on looks, it is important that you feel able to have a conversation about it. Listen to your child's concerns and don't dismiss them. It can be all too easy for you as a mum to say 'Don't be silly, you aren't fat,' but it is important to listen to what specific hang-ups your child has and why they make him feel a certain way.

Acne

For children, the common hang-up when it comes to skin is acne. Your child may repeatedly check her skin in the mirror, squeeze at any spots or go to great lengths to try and cover them up. She may look to you or other people to reassure her that her skin is fine and that the spots are not too noticeable. She may be intensely distressed by her appearance and it might get in the way of her being able to go to school or to socialize outside it. It might get in the way of her relationships with family or friends. Your child may constantly make excuses why he can't go anywhere and spend prolonged periods inside.

Ask your child where the idea has come from. Has someone said something to her? Has he been comparing himself to images on social media?

Your child may be preoccupied with specific body parts; skin, body shape and hair are commonly focused on.

Body dysmorphic disorder (BDD)

When your child has a particular hang-up, such as the colour of her skin or size of her nose, reassurance from friends and family may not be enough to placate her. She may repeatedly go to the doctor to try and find a way to change her perceived flaw. She may request to be referred to a specialist and try a whole host of treatments, but feel that none of these has been particularly successful in sorting the problem. BDD is more than just insecurity; it will cause your child to feel incredibly anxious and distressed about her perceived 'defect' and can be extremely disruptive to her day-to-day routine. She may stop going out as a result of it. The supposed defect may affect her personal and family relationships and may impact on things like school attendance due to a fear that attention will be drawn to it.

Gendered body hang-ups

As boys go through puberty, they may be more conscious of things like the size of their manhood or how big their muscles are compared to their friends. They may repeatedly look at themselves in the mirror, flexing their muscles. For girls, it may be the size of their chest, or a preoccupation with the fat around their thighs, hips or bum.

Whatever it is, your child may spend hours, days even, worrying about their 'imperfection'. I'm sure many of you reading this have thought there are times when you yourself have found fault with your appearance or had a complex about a specific body part and wondered whether you have body dysmorphia. Where do you draw the line? When does it stop being a lack of confidence and start becoming a mental illness? Generally, when we have negative thoughts about ourselves, we are to an extent able to shake these feelings off and get on with the demands of everyday life. People mistake body dysmorphia for a type of vanity, when that is simply not the case. It can be a hugely debilitating and distressing illness for your child.

It is highly likely that your child will not admit that there is a problem. It might come from you observing subsequent behaviours to body dysmorphia, such as social avoidance or poor school attendance.

Parents and carers can often feel frustrated if their child is exhibiting signs of BDD. They may ask their child to snap out of it or pull herself together. Despite your frustrations, it is important to remain calm and sensitive towards your child. BDD is something that will likely continue unless your child seeks some sort of professional help for it. It rarely gets better on its own.

Avoiding collusion

It is important that you do not 'collude' with your child if she has body image issues. By that I mean, if your child insists on repeatedly checking herself in a mirror and requests that you buy her an additional mirror, do not be swayed into doing so. By giving in you may be reinforcing your child's thoughts about her perceived flaw.

It is particularly important to maintain parental boundaries if your child is trying to find alternative solutions such as having surgery to achieve his perceived ideal. Helping your child access private surgeons and funding the surgery will not be helpful in the long term. What it inevitably does is fuel what is already a vicious cycle. Surgery does not solve the problem. Even after reconstructive surgery, your child may well be unsatisfied with the outcome and have the procedures unnecessarily repeated.

Taking puberty into account

Puberty can be a particularly difficult time for both boys and girls. Your child may feel that he is not in control of what is going on. She may lack understanding or may be unprepared for the bodily changes to come. For boys, there is the embarrassment of their voice breaking and of sprouting facial and body hair. For girls, suddenly developing breasts and experiencing their first period can be particularly difficult transition points. We know that even for children who do not have mental health issues, their mood can fluctuate around this time.

Your child may struggle with gains in weight around the time of puberty. Perhaps she has had a growth spurt and feels like the odd one out compared to her peers as she towers above them.

Dr Vohra's take-home messages: body image issues

- Despite any frustrations, it is important to remain calm and sensitive towards your child with BDD. BDD is something that will likely continue unless your child seeks some sort of professional help for it.
- Maintain parental boundaries, particularly in cases where your child may be trying to find alternative solutions such as surgery.
- For your child to have a fair shot at recovery, he needs to be able to access appropriate psychological support, whether that be an individual talking therapy or one that involves the whole family. By involving the family, the therapist may look at ways they can support the child to accept the perceived flaw without colluding with him or putting strain on the family unit.

Traffic light: green

FACE-FEAR

- Have a face-to-face conversation with your child.
- Be attentive; listen to what your child has to say.
- Stay calm.
- Explain to your child why you are worried.
- Agree an action and, if appropriate, go to amber.

Traffic light: amber

If you are concerned that your own child, or another child you know, is showing signs of BDD, then book an appointment with your GP.

Traffic light: red

Sometimes your child's symptoms may mean that he has thoughts of hurting himself or other people. The child may have actually acted on these thoughts and self-harmed; if he is known to have self-harmed already, you may have noticed that there is an increase in his self-harming behaviour. If you are concerned that your child is at risk of hurting himself or others, then ensure you seek support promptly. Contact the emergency services or take your child to A&E for an urgent assessment.

19

'I'm worried my child has gender difficulties'

There seems to be a lot in the media about gender identity and the struggles some children have in identifying themselves as the sex or gender they were born. Obviously, as children grow up, parents expect their children to go through various experimental phases, from what they wear and how they do their hair to their taste in music. One thing that parents expect will be fairly constant, however, is whether their child recognizes himself or herself to be a boy or a girl. Your daughter may be interested in trains or getting dirty or your son may be interested in fashion or straightening his hair, but you would always assume this meant that your child was a bit of a tomboy or a metrosexual or gay. It can come as a huge shock to parents when a child expresses confusion over his or her gender.

How fixed is the idea?

What distinguishes a child who is just being experimental from one with true gender identity difficulties is how fixed the belief is and the level of distress associated with it. Your child may have already started 'identifying' herself as a member of the opposite sex. She may insist that family refer to her by a particular name. A girl may start dressing as a boy or a boy as a girl. Your child may insist on using toilets or other areas appropriate to his desired sex. The child may play with toys that are intended for her preferred gender.

Although contemporary society has more of a focus on the need to be gender neutral, there are certain toys that we as parents associate more with one sex than another. Parents may find it odd to find their eight-year-old boy preferentially playing with dolls as opposed to cars.

Puberty

Often, if your child has gender identity difficulties, these will become even more distressing around the time of puberty. A girl who has expressed a wish to be a boy will feel very distressed when she starts to show obvious signs of becoming a woman, such as developing breasts or having her first period. For boys who want to transition to being girls, their voice breaking or the development of facial or chest hair might be a distressingly stark reminder of the gender they are trying to dissociate from.

Gender identity

Developmentally your child will normally know from an early age (between the ages of two and four) whether he or she is a boy or a girl. From this point, the behaviour the child shows will normally be in line with what you would expect of that gender. If your ten-year-old boy has throughout his life always referred to himself as a female, you can say with a degree of certainty that he could be experiencing difficulties with his gender identity.

Gender or sexuality?

A common misconception with respect to gender difficulties is that your child is probably not confused about her gender but about her sexuality; that is simply not the case. It can be really frustrating for your child when this conclusion is drawn. Yes, your child may identify himself or herself as a boy or a girl, but this does not necessarily mean the child will be attracted to the opposite sex as a result. Gender does not determine sexuality.

Parental worries

It can be a really difficult time for parents watching their child try to make sense of his or her gender identity. A lot of feelings may be stirred up within you as a parent. Why me? Is there something that I have done wrong? You may feel guilty that your child is experiencing this confusion. You may feel angry towards your child for putting you through this. Parents may blame themselves for being too liberal with their children, but gender identity issues are not a reflection on what you did or didn't do as a parent.

Parents may go through the stages of a grieving process as they come to terms with losing their son or daughter, the child they brought up. It can be a difficult and emotional journey for parents to go through.

A child's gender identity issues may affect not only the parents but also other relationships within the family. If you have other children, they may act out in a bid to bring some attention back to them.

Dr Vohra's take-home messages: gender identity

- Don't confuse gender identity with sexuality. Just because your child identifies him- or herself with a particular gender does not mean the child is attracted to the opposite sex as a result.
- Be mindful that puberty can often exacerbate your child's struggles with his or her gender identity.

FACE-FEAR

- If you suspect that your child may be struggling with his or her gender identity, try to have a face-to-face conversation with the child about it.
- Make sure you listen to what your child has to say. Don't be afraid to ask questions.
- Stay calm.
- Your child may open up to you the first time you speak to him or it may take several conversations to get anything out of him. It is important to remain patient and not rush your child.
- If you are concerned, seek advice from your child's GP.

20

What to expect: the first appointment with a GP or psychiatrist

Every parent worries their child will develop a mental health condition. Parents feel a real sense of responsibility when their child's struggles come to light, but many other factors that we as doctors consider go far beyond what happens within the family. Yes, family is an important factor, but it is not the only factor.

Parents often panic that a family history of a mental health condition will make it more likely that it is passed down to younger generations. It is important to bear in mind that not all mental health conditions depend solely on genetics. Believe it or not, our environment - the world we live in, who we have grown up with, what we have experienced within our lives, to give just a few examples - have just as important a role to play.

If you are a foster carer, a step-parent or a parent who has adopted a child, you may not be fully aware of the mental health backgrounds of those in your son or daughter's extended biological family. This uncertainty can be quite a worrisome thought for some parents. Furthermore, you may consider how your own behaviours or mental health difficulties may affect your child. For instance, a step-parent with severe OCD that renders him housebound for the majority of the time may commonly worry that his checking behaviours and rituals will be 'inherited' by his child.

Whatever your concerns may be, your GP or psychiatrist is the person best placed to explore them with you. At the initial appointment, your GP will want to take a full medical and psychiatric history. This will cover everything from why you have brought your child to see the GP today right through to whether your child has ever been in trouble with the police. The whole process can seem like a lengthy one, but looking at the minutiae will help us, as healthcare professionals, put your child's difficulties into context and try to piece together why this has happened to your child in the first place, and why now.

Questions at the first appointment

This chapter look at the sorts of things we would normally want to know at that all-important first appointment. By using it as a reference, you can walk into the appointment feeling more prepared to answer any questions that, in hindsight, you could have done with longer to mull over.

What is the 'problem' or 'difficulty'?

The first thing your doctor will want to know is why you have brought your child to see her. What is the specific problem or difficulty that you are concerned about? Another obvious question, is what has happened for you to have brought your child in today, as opposed to yesterday or tomorrow?

Articulate your uncertainty

Some parents can give a clear timeline of when their worries started and what specifically they are worried about. Others find it difficult to articulate exactly what their concerns are. It may be that, as a parent, you just know that something is not quite right but are at a loss as to what to do. If your gut instinct is telling you something is not quite right, have the confidence to tell your doctor this. Your doctor ought to listen to and validate your concerns.

How long has it been going on for?

When you notice a change in your child's behaviour, you might have a think about *how long it has gone on for.* You may not be able to pin it down to a particular date and time, but have a think: has the change taken place over a number of days, weeks, months or years?

Is it getting worse or better?

Your doctor will be interested in what we call the 'course' of your child's symptoms. By that we mean, since you noticed that there was a problem, have the symptoms got worse, better or stayed about the same? It might be that what started out as one problem – say, low mood – has turned into several difficulties by the time you get to see your GP.

Have you noticed a pattern to the problem?

There are so many factors that may affect your child's mood and behaviour. It may be that certain things make your child's symptoms worse. As an example, symptoms such as low mood may be worse in the morning or your child's voices may be more sinister at night. You might notice patterns for the better. For instance, it might be that your child's mood improves when she is around other people.

Is there anything you can think of that has contributed to the problem?

This can be anything from fallings-out within the family to difficulties at school. It might be that your child has experienced something really traumatic in his life. He may have been involved in a road traffic accident, witnessed his mum being beaten up by his dad or he may be a victim of abuse himself.

Your child may be going through a significant school transition. She may have just started at nursery, she may have recently joined a primary or secondary school. Perhaps you have recently moved house or out of the area where your child was brought up and he is having to face up to the prospect of a complete new beginning.

How are things at school?

Does your child enjoy school? Has there been a change in her attitude towards school? Does she have a good circle of friends? Is she being bullied? Has there been a change in her academic performance? School report cards and parents' evenings are useful ways to track your child's progress. Have his marks slipped? Are you hearing from teachers more often? Perhaps you generally don't hear from your child's school in between parents' evenings, but more recently you are finding that trips to the school to meet the head are becoming more frequent.

An important thing to consider when communicating with your child's school is what the child's behaviour is like once she is there. Obviously school staff are best placed to answer this. Are the teachers concerned that the child is more withdrawn than normal? Have they noticed that she has lost weight or been more unruly and disruptive? Have there been multiple exclusions? Can you be sure that the child is attending school at all? Is she truanting?

How are things at home?

Looking at your child's difficulties in the context of what is going on at home is invaluable. Your GP or healthcare professional may ask you to go through a family tree, a who's who of the family. Is the family environment a happy one or have there been a lot of struggles recently? Family disharmony can often affect a young person's mental state. Parents and carers often find it difficult to share the ins and outs of what is happening in the home environment. It can often feel intrusive; families worry that they will be judged by healthcare professionals. It may leave you feeling vulnerable, as if nothing is sacred, but the more information we can glean from you the better. This allows us to fully understand your child in the context of what is going on at home, which invariably is where children spend most of their time.

What is the dynamic like at home? Has there been a change recently? Any parental discord? Are parents going through a separation? Is your child struggling with the blending of families? Are financial stresses affecting the whole family?

Has there been a change in the child's relationships?

Often we expect that, as children go through their teenage years, they will fall in and out of friendships and relationships. You may notice a change in friendships for the worse; you may find your child hanging out with unsavoury characters. Maybe you used to have a good, open relationship with your child, but recently she has become a lot more secretive. All this information may not necessarily be considered relevant by you, but collectively it is really helpful for us when putting your child's difficulties into context.

Has the child experienced anything like this before?

It may be that your child had trouble with her mood a few years ago but it subsided and there had not been a problem again until fairly recently.

Has the child been under a mental health team in the past?

If so, what did or didn't work? Perhaps the child had some talking therapy and didn't find it helpful, but may now be in a position where he wants to think about it again.

How is the child's physical health?

Does your child have any chronic illnesses? Does he see the GP for anything?

Is the child on any medication?

This may be medication for either physical or mental health. Your child may be taking regular over-the-counter medication for an ailment. Has there been any recent change in medication - new medication started, changes in dose or medication stopped - that could explain the child's symptoms?

Does anyone in the family have any mental health difficulties?

This is one of the important things that a healthcare professional will want to clarify. Just because a member of the family suffers with a mental disorder does not automatically mean that it will be passed down to your child, but a family history of mental illness means it may be more likely that your child could develop these symptoms.

Development

The doctor will be interested to learn about your child's development. She may ask you questions that seem irrelevant, but there is a lot of evidence suggesting that early development does impact on us as individuals, our interactions with other people and how we see the world.

Your pregnancy and the birth of your child

Your child's GP or psychiatrist will most likely be interested in how the pregnancy and subsequent birth went. Was it uneventful or were there any difficulties in the antenatal period? Was it a normal delivery or a caesarean? Was there any trauma during delivery? How much did the baby weigh? Did it need any time on a special care baby unit?

The early days

How was your child's development? Did she reach all her milestones on time? Any problems with feeding? What about weaning? Was your child walking and talking at the times expected for her age? How did the child get on at nursery? Would she play with other children or share toys?

Remembering the little details

You would be surprised at how often parents need to rack their brains to think about the minutiae of the pregnancy and the early years. Do you have your child's red book to hand? If so, this can be a valuable resource for healthcare professionals.

Other information that we may want to know

Has your child ever been in trouble with the police? Does she smoke, drink or use illegal drugs? If so, how long has she done so?

Dr Vohra's take-home messages: the first appointment

- Keep hold of your child's red book.
- Keep a mental note or jot down your experience of pregnancy and your child's early years.
- Keep hold of any school report cards.
- Have a think about significant things that have happened to your child, both in early childhood and more recently.

A final note

If you have read this far, it is only natural that you may be feeling overwhelmed – we have covered a lot of ground and discussed a lot of difficult topics. Rest assured, however, it is unlikely that your child, during her lifetime, will experience all of the conditions mentioned, but I hope this book will give you a strong foundation of knowledge and get you thinking about the sorts of emotional struggles your child may experience. If you have found yourself nodding along in recognition at various points, then I hope that the practical tips on communication, symptom breakdowns and closing checklists have helped bring your own concerns to the surface and instilled in you the confidence to discuss such matters with your child and agree on an action plan together.

It can be natural as a parent to feel guilty about your child's struggles with her mental health. Often the situation isn't helped when your child does not want, or feel able, to communicate with you; this can often be a representation of how entrenched her mental health difficulties have become. It is important not to take this as a reflection on what you are or are not doing as a parent.

It can be easy to forget, in all of this, about your own emotional well-being. Watching your child experience what at times can be extremely difficult emotions is bound to have a knock-on effect on you. Your every waking moment may be consumed with guilt and feelings of helplessness. You may have experienced mental health difficulties yourself in the past or you may be struggling with them currently. If that is the case, observing your child's distress can often trigger your own, so it is crucial that you have a strong, steady support network around you, whether this is in the form of friends, family members or professionals. By looking after your own emotional well-being, you free up capacity to listen and process what is happening in the life of your child.

If you take away just one message from this book, let it be the importance of communication and FACE-ing the FEAR of mental health. Tackle it head on, be attentive, keep calm, find out the facts, explain your concerns, agree on actions and review. With a combination of these simple steps, a little compassion and swift access to professional advice, you won't go far wrong.

Index